C-1527 CAREER EXAMINATION SERIES

This is your
PASSBOOK for...

Urban Designer

Test Preparation Study Guide
Questions & Answers

NATIONAL LEARNING CORPORATION®

COPYRIGHT NOTICE

This book is SOLELY intended for, is sold ONLY to, and its use is RESTRICTED to individual, bona fide applicants or candidates who qualify by virtue of having seriously filed applications for appropriate license, certificate, professional and/or promotional advancement, higher school matriculation, scholarship, or other legitimate requirements of education and/or governmental authorities.

This book is NOT intended for use, class instruction, tutoring, training, duplication, copying, reprinting, excerption, or adaptation, etc., by:

1) Other publishers
2) Proprietors and/or Instructors of "Coaching" and/or Preparatory Courses
3) Personnel and/or Training Divisions of commercial, industrial, and governmental organizations
4) Schools, colleges, or universities and/or their departments and staffs, including teachers and other personnel
5) Testing Agencies or Bureaus
6) Study groups which seek by the purchase of a single volume to copy and/or duplicate and/or adapt this material for use by the group as a whole without having purchased individual volumes for each of the members of the group
7) Et al.

Such persons would be in violation of appropriate Federal and State statutes.

PROVISION OF LICENSING AGREEMENTS – Recognized educational, commercial, industrial, and governmental institutions and organizations, and others legitimately engaged in educational pursuits, including training, testing, and measurement activities, may address request for a licensing agreement to the copyright owners, who will determine whether, and under what conditions, including fees and charges, the materials in this book may be used them. In other words, a licensing facility exists for the legitimate use of the material in this book on other than an individual basis. However, it is asseverated and affirmed here that the material in this book CANNOT be used without the receipt of the express permission of such a licensing agreement from the Publishers. Inquiries re licensing should be addressed to the company, attention rights and permissions department.

All rights reserved, including the right of reproduction in whole or in part, in any form or by any means, electronic or mechanical, including photocopying, recording, or by any information storage and retrieval system, without permission in writing from the Publisher.

Copyright © 2025 by
National Learning Corporation

212 Michael Drive, Syosset, NY 11791
(516) 921-8888 • www.passbooks.com
E-mail: info@passbooks.com

PASSBOOK® SERIES

THE *PASSBOOK® SERIES* has been created to prepare applicants and candidates for the ultimate academic battlefield – the examination room.

At some time in our lives, each and every one of us may be required to take an examination – for validation, matriculation, admission, qualification, registration, certification, or licensure.

Based on the assumption that every applicant or candidate has met the basic formal educational standards, has taken the required number of courses, and read the necessary texts, the *PASSBOOK® SERIES* furnishes the one special preparation which may assure passing with confidence, instead of failing with insecurity. Examination questions – together with answers – are furnished as the basic vehicle for study so that the mysteries of the examination and its compounding difficulties may be eliminated or diminished by a sure method.

This book is meant to help you pass your examination provided that you qualify and are serious in your objective.

The entire field is reviewed through the huge store of content information which is succinctly presented through a provocative and challenging approach – the question-and-answer method.

A climate of success is established by furnishing the correct answers at the end of each test.

You soon learn to recognize types of questions, forms of questions, and patterns of questioning. You may even begin to anticipate expected outcomes.

You perceive that many questions are repeated or adapted so that you can gain acute insights, which may enable you to score many sure points.

You learn how to confront new questions, or types of questions, and to attack them confidently and work out the correct answers.

You note objectives and emphases, and recognize pitfalls and dangers, so that you may make positive educational adjustments.

Moreover, you are kept fully informed in relation to new concepts, methods, practices, and directions in the field.

You discover that you are actually taking the examination all the time: you are preparing for the examination by "taking" an examination, not by reading extraneous and/or supererogatory textbooks.

In short, this PASSBOOK®, used directedly, should be an important factor in helping you to pass your test.

URBAN DESIGNER

DUTIES AND RESPONSIBILITIES
Under general supervision, performs difficult and responsible work in urban design; may supervise subordinate personnel; performs related work.

EXAMPLES OF TYPICAL TASKS
Supervises a small squad, unit, or group engaged in the performance of urban design and related work.
Engages in or supervises the conduct of complex and important research investigations, studies or examinations related to the assessment of the physical design implications of the major geographic features, transportation net, basic land use patterns and neighborhood structures. Prepares analyses of the spatial organization and efficient utilization of sites and structures. Within prescribed limits, initiates urban design concepts. Prepares detailed neighborhood and area urban design plans. Prepares or supervises the preparation of drawings relating to urban design development studies; carries out urban design development studies.

TESTS
The test may include questions on urban design concepts and methods of implementation, including urban renewal design controls, special zoning districts, design review procedures, and site selection criteria; architectural design concepts, including knowledge of characteristics of various building types; knowledge of government and functions, codes and regulations that affect urban design (including zoning and mapping), and role of community in planning and urban design decisions; supervisory and administrative skills, including organization planning and design studies, assigning and supervising portions of work programs; and other related areas.

HOW TO TAKE A TEST

I. YOU MUST PASS AN EXAMINATION

A. *WHAT EVERY CANDIDATE SHOULD KNOW*

Examination applicants often ask us for help in preparing for the written test. What can I study in advance? What kinds of questions will be asked? How will the test be given? How will the papers be graded?

As an applicant for a civil service examination, you may be wondering about some of these things. Our purpose here is to suggest effective methods of advance study and to describe civil service examinations.

Your chances for success on this examination can be increased if you know how to prepare. Those "pre-examination jitters" can be reduced if you know what to expect. You can even experience an adventure in good citizenship if you know why civil service exams are given.

B. *WHY ARE CIVIL SERVICE EXAMINATIONS GIVEN?*

Civil service examinations are important to you in two ways. As a citizen, you want public jobs filled by employees who know how to do their work. As a job seeker, you want a fair chance to compete for that job on an equal footing with other candidates. The best-known means of accomplishing this two-fold goal is the competitive examination.

Exams are widely publicized throughout the nation. They may be administered for jobs in federal, state, city, municipal, town or village governments or agencies.

Any citizen may apply, with some limitations, such as the age or residence of applicants. Your experience and education may be reviewed to see whether you meet the requirements for the particular examination. When these requirements exist, they are reasonable and applied consistently to all applicants. Thus, a competitive examination may cause you some uneasiness now, but it is your privilege and safeguard.

C. *HOW ARE CIVIL SERVICE EXAMS DEVELOPED?*

Examinations are carefully written by trained technicians who are specialists in the field known as "psychological measurement," in consultation with recognized authorities in the field of work that the test will cover. These experts recommend the subject matter areas or skills to be tested; only those knowledges or skills important to your success on the job are included. The most reliable books and source materials available are used as references. Together, the experts and technicians judge the difficulty level of the questions.

Test technicians know how to phrase questions so that the problem is clearly stated. Their ethics do not permit "trick" or "catch" questions. Questions may have been tried out on sample groups, or subjected to statistical analysis, to determine their usefulness.

Written tests are often used in combination with performance tests, ratings of training and experience, and oral interviews. All of these measures combine to form the best-known means of finding the right person for the right job.

II. HOW TO PASS THE WRITTEN TEST

A. NATURE OF THE EXAMINATION

To prepare intelligently for civil service examinations, you should know how they differ from school examinations you have taken. In school you were assigned certain definite pages to read or subjects to cover. The examination questions were quite detailed and usually emphasized memory. Civil service exams, on the other hand, try to discover your present ability to perform the duties of a position, plus your potentiality to learn these duties. In other words, a civil service exam attempts to predict how successful you will be. Questions cover such a broad area that they cannot be as minute and detailed as school exam questions.

In the public service similar kinds of work, or positions, are grouped together in one "class." This process is known as *position-classification*. All the positions in a class are paid according to the salary range for that class. One class title covers all of these positions, and they are all tested by the same examination.

B. FOUR BASIC STEPS

1) Study the announcement

How, then, can you know what subjects to study? Our best answer is: "Learn as much as possible about the class of positions for which you've applied." The exam will test the knowledge, skills and abilities needed to do the work.

Your most valuable source of information about the position you want is the official exam announcement. This announcement lists the training and experience qualifications. Check these standards and apply only if you come reasonably close to meeting them.

The brief description of the position in the examination announcement offers some clues to the subjects which will be tested. Think about the job itself. Review the duties in your mind. Can you perform them, or are there some in which you are rusty? Fill in the blank spots in your preparation.

Many jurisdictions preview the written test in the exam announcement by including a section called "Knowledge and Abilities Required," "Scope of the Examination," or some similar heading. Here you will find out specifically what fields will be tested.

2) Review your own background

Once you learn in general what the position is all about, and what you need to know to do the work, ask yourself which subjects you already know fairly well and which need improvement. You may wonder whether to concentrate on improving your strong areas or on building some background in your fields of weakness. When the announcement has specified "some knowledge" or "considerable knowledge," or has used adjectives like "beginning principles of…" or "advanced … methods," you can get a clue as to the number and difficulty of questions to be asked in any given field. More questions, and hence broader coverage, would be included for those subjects which are more important in the work. Now weigh your strengths and weaknesses against the job requirements and prepare accordingly.

3) Determine the level of the position

Another way to tell how intensively you should prepare is to understand the level of the job for which you are applying. Is it the entering level? In other words, is this the position in which beginners in a field of work are hired? Or is it an intermediate or advanced level? Sometimes this is indicated by such words as "Junior" or "Senior" in the class title. Other jurisdictions use Roman numerals to designate the level – Clerk I, Clerk II, for example. The word "Supervisor" sometimes appears in the title. If the level is not indicated by the title, check the description of duties. Will you be working under very close supervision, or will you have responsibility for independent decisions in this work?

4) Choose appropriate study materials

Now that you know the subjects to be examined and the relative amount of each subject to be covered, you can choose suitable study materials. For beginning level jobs, or even advanced ones, if you have a pronounced weakness in some aspect of your training, read a modern, standard textbook in that field. Be sure it is up to date and has general coverage. Such books are normally available at your library, and the librarian will be glad to help you locate one. For entry-level positions, questions of appropriate difficulty are chosen – neither highly advanced questions, nor those too simple. Such questions require careful thought but not advanced training.

If the position for which you are applying is technical or advanced, you will read more advanced, specialized material. If you are already familiar with the basic principles of your field, elementary textbooks would waste your time. Concentrate on advanced textbooks and technical periodicals. Think through the concepts and review difficult problems in your field.

These are all general sources. You can get more ideas on your own initiative, following these leads. For example, training manuals and publications of the government agency which employs workers in your field can be useful, particularly for technical and professional positions. A letter or visit to the government department involved may result in more specific study suggestions, and certainly will provide you with a more definite idea of the exact nature of the position you are seeking.

III. KINDS OF TESTS

Tests are used for purposes other than measuring knowledge and ability to perform specified duties. For some positions, it is equally important to test ability to make adjustments to new situations or to profit from training. In others, basic mental abilities not dependent on information are essential. Questions which test these things may not appear as pertinent to the duties of the position as those which test for knowledge and information. Yet they are often highly important parts of a fair examination. For very general questions, it is almost impossible to help you direct your study efforts. What we can do is to point out some of the more common of these general abilities needed in public service positions and describe some typical questions.

1) General information

Broad, general information has been found useful for predicting job success in some kinds of work. This is tested in a variety of ways, from vocabulary lists to questions about current events. Basic background in some field of work, such as sociology or economics, may be sampled in a group of questions. Often these are principles which have become familiar to most persons through exposure rather than through formal training. It is difficult to advise you how to study for these questions; being alert to the world around you is our best suggestion.

2) Verbal ability

An example of an ability needed in many positions is verbal or language ability. Verbal ability is, in brief, the ability to use and understand words. Vocabulary and grammar tests are typical measures of this ability. Reading comprehension or paragraph interpretation questions are common in many kinds of civil service tests. You are given a paragraph of written material and asked to find its central meaning.

3) Numerical ability

Number skills can be tested by the familiar arithmetic problem, by checking paired lists of numbers to see which are alike and which are different, or by interpreting charts and graphs. In the latter test, a graph may be printed in the test booklet which you are asked to use as the basis for answering questions.

4) Observation

A popular test for law-enforcement positions is the observation test. A picture is shown to you for several minutes, then taken away. Questions about the picture test your ability to observe both details and larger elements.

5) Following directions

In many positions in the public service, the employee must be able to carry out written instructions dependably and accurately. You may be given a chart with several columns, each column listing a variety of information. The questions require you to carry out directions involving the information given in the chart.

6) Skills and aptitudes

Performance tests effectively measure some manual skills and aptitudes. When the skill is one in which you are trained, such as typing or shorthand, you can practice. These tests are often very much like those given in business school or high school courses. For many of the other skills and aptitudes, however, no short-time preparation can be made. Skills and abilities natural to you or that you have developed throughout your lifetime are being tested.

Many of the general questions just described provide all the data needed to answer the questions and ask you to use your reasoning ability to find the answers. Your best preparation for these tests, as well as for tests of facts and ideas, is to be at your physical and mental best. You, no doubt, have your own methods of getting into an exam-taking mood and keeping "in shape." The next section lists some ideas on this subject.

IV. KINDS OF QUESTIONS

Only rarely is the "essay" question, which you answer in narrative form, used in civil service tests. Civil service tests are usually of the short-answer type. Full instructions for answering these questions will be given to you at the examination. But in case this is your first experience with short-answer questions and separate answer sheets, here is what you need to know:

1) Multiple-choice Questions

Most popular of the short-answer questions is the "multiple choice" or "best answer" question. It can be used, for example, to test for factual knowledge, ability to solve problems or judgment in meeting situations found at work.

A multiple-choice question is normally one of three types—
- It can begin with an incomplete statement followed by several possible endings. You are to find the one ending which *best* completes the statement, although some of the others may not be entirely wrong.
- It can also be a complete statement in the form of a question which is answered by choosing one of the statements listed.

- It can be in the form of a problem – again you select the best answer.

Here is an example of a multiple-choice question with a discussion which should give you some clues as to the method for choosing the right answer:

When an employee has a complaint about his assignment, the action which will *best* help him overcome his difficulty is to
- A. discuss his difficulty with his coworkers
- B. take the problem to the head of the organization
- C. take the problem to the person who gave him the assignment
- D. say nothing to anyone about his complaint

In answering this question, you should study each of the choices to find which is best. Consider choice "A" – Certainly an employee may discuss his complaint with fellow employees, but no change or improvement can result, and the complaint remains unresolved. Choice "B" is a poor choice since the head of the organization probably does not know what assignment you have been given, and taking your problem to him is known as "going over the head" of the supervisor. The supervisor, or person who made the assignment, is the person who can clarify it or correct any injustice. Choice "C" is, therefore, correct. To say nothing, as in choice "D," is unwise. Supervisors have and interest in knowing the problems employees are facing, and the employee is seeking a solution to his problem.

2) True/False Questions

The "true/false" or "right/wrong" form of question is sometimes used. Here a complete statement is given. Your job is to decide whether the statement is right or wrong.

SAMPLE: A roaming cell-phone call to a nearby city costs less than a non-roaming call to a distant city.

This statement is wrong, or false, since roaming calls are more expensive.

This is not a complete list of all possible question forms, although most of the others are variations of these common types. You will always get complete directions for answering questions. Be sure you understand *how* to mark your answers – ask questions until you do.

V. RECORDING YOUR ANSWERS

Computer terminals are used more and more today for many different kinds of exams.
For an examination with very few applicants, you may be told to record your answers in the test booklet itself. Separate answer sheets are much more common. If this separate answer sheet is to be scored by machine – and this is often the case – it is highly important that you mark your answers correctly in order to get credit.

An electronic scoring machine is often used in civil service offices because of the speed with which papers can be scored. Machine-scored answer sheets must be marked with a pencil, which will be given to you. This pencil has a high graphite content which responds to the electronic scoring machine. As a matter of fact, stray dots may register as answers, so do not let your pencil rest on the answer sheet while you are pondering the correct answer. Also, if your pencil lead breaks or is otherwise defective, ask for another.

Since the answer sheet will be dropped in a slot in the scoring machine, be careful not to bend the corners or get the paper crumpled.

The answer sheet normally has five vertical columns of numbers, with 30 numbers to a column. These numbers correspond to the question numbers in your test booklet. After each number, going across the page are four or five pairs of dotted lines. These short dotted lines have small letters or numbers above them. The first two pairs may also have a "T" or "F" above the letters. This indicates that the first two pairs only are to be used if the questions are of the true-false type. If the questions are multiple choice, disregard the "T" and "F" and pay attention only to the small letters or numbers.

Answer your questions in the manner of the sample that follows:

32. The largest city in the United States is
   A. Washington, D.C.
   B. New York City
   C. Chicago
   D. Detroit
   E. San Francisco

1) Choose the answer you think is best. (New York City is the largest, so "B" is correct.)
2) Find the row of dotted lines numbered the same as the question you are answering. (Find row number 32)
3) Find the pair of dotted lines corresponding to the answer. (Find the pair of lines under the mark "B.")
4) Make a solid black mark between the dotted lines.

VI. BEFORE THE TEST

Common sense will help you find procedures to follow to get ready for an examination. Too many of us, however, overlook these sensible measures. Indeed, nervousness and fatigue have been found to be the most serious reasons why applicants fail to do their best on civil service tests. Here is a list of reminders:

- Begin your preparation early – Don't wait until the last minute to go scurrying around for books and materials or to find out what the position is all about.
- Prepare continuously – An hour a night for a week is better than an all-night cram session. This has been definitely established. What is more, a night a week for a month will return better dividends than crowding your study into a shorter period of time.
- Locate the place of the exam – You have been sent a notice telling you when and where to report for the examination. If the location is in a different town or otherwise unfamiliar to you, it would be well to inquire the best route and learn something about the building.
- Relax the night before the test – Allow your mind to rest. Do not study at all that night. Plan some mild recreation or diversion; then go to bed early and get a good night's sleep.
- Get up early enough to make a leisurely trip to the place for the test – This way unforeseen events, traffic snarls, unfamiliar buildings, etc. will not upset you.
- Dress comfortably – A written test is not a fashion show. You will be known by number and not by name, so wear something comfortable.

- Leave excess paraphernalia at home – Shopping bags and odd bundles will get in your way. You need bring only the items mentioned in the official notice you received; usually everything you need is provided. Do not bring reference books to the exam. They will only confuse those last minutes and be taken away from you when in the test room.
- Arrive somewhat ahead of time – If because of transportation schedules you must get there very early, bring a newspaper or magazine to take your mind off yourself while waiting.
- Locate the examination room – When you have found the proper room, you will be directed to the seat or part of the room where you will sit. Sometimes you are given a sheet of instructions to read while you are waiting. Do not fill out any forms until you are told to do so; just read them and be prepared.
- Relax and prepare to listen to the instructions
- If you have any physical problem that may keep you from doing your best, be sure to tell the test administrator. If you are sick or in poor health, you really cannot do your best on the exam. You can come back and take the test some other time.

VII. AT THE TEST

The day of the test is here and you have the test booklet in your hand. The temptation to get going is very strong. Caution! There is more to success than knowing the right answers. You must know how to identify your papers and understand variations in the type of short-answer question used in this particular examination. Follow these suggestions for maximum results from your efforts:

1) Cooperate with the monitor

The test administrator has a duty to create a situation in which you can be as much at ease as possible. He will give instructions, tell you when to begin, check to see that you are marking your answer sheet correctly, and so on. He is not there to guard you, although he will see that your competitors do not take unfair advantage. He wants to help you do your best.

2) Listen to all instructions

Don't jump the gun! Wait until you understand all directions. In most civil service tests you get more time than you need to answer the questions. So don't be in a hurry. Read each word of instructions until you clearly understand the meaning. Study the examples, listen to all announcements and follow directions. Ask questions if you do not understand what to do.

3) Identify your papers

Civil service exams are usually identified by number only. You will be assigned a number; you must not put your name on your test papers. Be sure to copy your number correctly. Since more than one exam may be given, copy your exact examination title.

4) Plan your time

Unless you are told that a test is a "speed" or "rate of work" test, speed itself is usually not important. Time enough to answer all the questions will be provided, but this does not mean that you have all day. An overall time limit has been set. Divide the total time (in minutes) by the number of questions to determine the approximate time you have for each question.

5) Do not linger over difficult questions

If you come across a difficult question, mark it with a paper clip (useful to have along) and come back to it when you have been through the booklet. One caution if you do this – be sure to skip a number on your answer sheet as well. Check often to be sure that you have not lost your place and that you are marking in the row numbered the same as the question you are answering.

6) Read the questions

Be sure you know what the question asks! Many capable people are unsuccessful because they failed to *read* the questions correctly.

7) Answer all questions

Unless you have been instructed that a penalty will be deducted for incorrect answers, it is better to guess than to omit a question.

8) Speed tests

It is often better NOT to guess on speed tests. It has been found that on timed tests people are tempted to spend the last few seconds before time is called in marking answers at random – without even reading them – in the hope of picking up a few extra points. To discourage this practice, the instructions may warn you that your score will be "corrected" for guessing. That is, a penalty will be applied. The incorrect answers will be deducted from the correct ones, or some other penalty formula will be used.

9) Review your answers

If you finish before time is called, go back to the questions you guessed or omitted to give them further thought. Review other answers if you have time.

10) Return your test materials

If you are ready to leave before others have finished or time is called, take ALL your materials to the monitor and leave quietly. Never take any test material with you. The monitor can discover whose papers are not complete, and taking a test booklet may be grounds for disqualification.

VIII. EXAMINATION TECHNIQUES

1) Read the general instructions carefully. These are usually printed on the first page of the exam booklet. As a rule, these instructions refer to the timing of the examination; the fact that you should not start work until the signal and must stop work at a signal, etc. If there are any *special* instructions, such as a choice of questions to be answered, make sure that you note this instruction carefully.

2) When you are ready to start work on the examination, that is as soon as the signal has been given, read the instructions to each question booklet, underline any key words or phrases, such as *least, best, outline, describe* and the like. In this way you will tend to answer as requested rather than discover on reviewing your paper that you *listed without describing*, that you selected the *worst* choice rather than the *best* choice, etc.

3) If the examination is of the objective or multiple-choice type – that is, each question will also give a series of possible answers: A, B, C or D, and you are called upon to select the best answer and write the letter next to that answer on your answer paper – it is advisable to start answering each question in turn. There may be anywhere from 50 to 100 such questions in the three or four hours allotted and you can see how much time would be taken if you read through all the questions before beginning to answer any. Furthermore, if you come across a question or group of questions which you know would be difficult to answer, it would undoubtedly affect your handling of all the other questions.

4) If the examination is of the essay type and contains but a few questions, it is a moot point as to whether you should read all the questions before starting to answer any one. Of course, if you are given a choice – say five out of seven and the like – then it is essential to read all the questions so you can eliminate the two that are most difficult. If, however, you are asked to answer all the questions, there may be danger in trying to answer the easiest one first because you may find that you will spend too much time on it. The best technique is to answer the first question, then proceed to the second, etc.

5) Time your answers. Before the exam begins, write down the time it started, then add the time allowed for the examination and write down the time it must be completed, then divide the time available somewhat as follows:
    - If 3-1/2 hours are allowed, that would be 210 minutes. If you have 80 objective-type questions, that would be an average of 2-1/2 minutes per question. Allow yourself no more than 2 minutes per question, or a total of 160 minutes, which will permit about 50 minutes to review.
    - If for the time allotment of 210 minutes there are 7 essay questions to answer, that would average about 30 minutes a question. Give yourself only 25 minutes per question so that you have about 35 minutes to review.

6) The most important instruction is to *read each question* and make sure you know what is wanted. The second most important instruction is to *time yourself properly* so that you answer every question. The third most important instruction is to *answer every question*. Guess if you have to but include something for each question. Remember that you will receive no credit for a blank and will probably receive some credit if you write something in answer to an essay question. If you guess a letter – say "B" for a multiple-choice question – you may have guessed right. If you leave a blank as an answer to a multiple-choice question, the examiners may respect your feelings but it will not add a point to your score. Some exams may penalize you for wrong answers, so in such cases *only*, you may not want to guess unless you have some basis for your answer.

7) Suggestions
    a. Objective-type questions
        1. Examine the question booklet for proper sequence of pages and questions
        2. Read all instructions carefully
        3. Skip any question which seems too difficult; return to it after all other questions have been answered
        4. Apportion your time properly; do not spend too much time on any single question or group of questions

5. Note and underline key words – *all, most, fewest, least, best, worst, same, opposite,* etc.
6. Pay particular attention to negatives
7. Note unusual option, e.g., unduly long, short, complex, different or similar in content to the body of the question
8. Observe the use of "hedging" words – *probably, may, most likely,* etc.
9. Make sure that your answer is put next to the same number as the question
10. Do not second-guess unless you have good reason to believe the second answer is definitely more correct
11. Cross out original answer if you decide another answer is more accurate; do not erase until you are ready to hand your paper in
12. Answer all questions; guess unless instructed otherwise
13. Leave time for review

b. Essay questions
1. Read each question carefully
2. Determine exactly what is wanted. Underline key words or phrases.
3. Decide on outline or paragraph answer
4. Include many different points and elements unless asked to develop any one or two points or elements
5. Show impartiality by giving pros and cons unless directed to select one side only
6. Make and write down any assumptions you find necessary to answer the questions
7. Watch your English, grammar, punctuation and choice of words
8. Time your answers; don't crowd material

8) Answering the essay question

Most essay questions can be answered by framing the specific response around several key words or ideas. Here are a few such key words or ideas:

M's: manpower, materials, methods, money, management
P's: purpose, program, policy, plan, procedure, practice, problems, pitfalls, personnel, public relations

a. Six basic steps in handling problems:
1. Preliminary plan and background development
2. Collect information, data and facts
3. Analyze and interpret information, data and facts
4. Analyze and develop solutions as well as make recommendations
5. Prepare report and sell recommendations
6. Install recommendations and follow up effectiveness

b. Pitfalls to avoid
1. *Taking things for granted* – A statement of the situation does not necessarily imply that each of the elements is necessarily true; for example, a complaint may be invalid and biased so that all that can be taken for granted is that a complaint has been registered

2. *Considering only one side of a situation* – Wherever possible, indicate several alternatives and then point out the reasons you selected the best one
3. *Failing to indicate follow up* – Whenever your answer indicates action on your part, make certain that you will take proper follow-up action to see how successful your recommendations, procedures or actions turn out to be
4. *Taking too long in answering any single question* – Remember to time your answers properly

IX. AFTER THE TEST

Scoring procedures differ in detail among civil service jurisdictions although the general principles are the same. Whether the papers are hand-scored or graded by machine we have described, they are nearly always graded by number. That is, the person who marks the paper knows only the number – never the name – of the applicant. Not until all the papers have been graded will they be matched with names. If other tests, such as training and experience or oral interview ratings have been given, scores will be combined. Different parts of the examination usually have different weights. For example, the written test might count 60 percent of the final grade, and a rating of training and experience 40 percent. In many jurisdictions, veterans will have a certain number of points added to their grades.

After the final grade has been determined, the names are placed in grade order and an eligible list is established. There are various methods for resolving ties between those who get the same final grade – probably the most common is to place first the name of the person whose application was received first. Job offers are made from the eligible list in the order the names appear on it. You will be notified of your grade and your rank as soon as all these computations have been made. This will be done as rapidly as possible.

People who are found to meet the requirements in the announcement are called "eligibles." Their names are put on a list of eligible candidates. An eligible's chances of getting a job depend on how high he stands on this list and how fast agencies are filling jobs from the list.

When a job is to be filled from a list of eligibles, the agency asks for the names of people on the list of eligibles for that job. When the civil service commission receives this request, it sends to the agency the names of the three people highest on this list. Or, if the job to be filled has specialized requirements, the office sends the agency the names of the top three persons who meet these requirements from the general list.

The appointing officer makes a choice from among the three people whose names were sent to him. If the selected person accepts the appointment, the names of the others are put back on the list to be considered for future openings.

That is the rule in hiring from all kinds of eligible lists, whether they are for typist, carpenter, chemist, or something else. For every vacancy, the appointing officer has his choice of any one of the top three eligibles on the list. This explains why the person whose name is on top of the list sometimes does not get an appointment when some of the persons lower on the list do. If the appointing officer chooses the second or third eligible, the No. 1 eligible does not get a job at once, but stays on the list until he is appointed or the list is terminated.

X. HOW TO PASS THE INTERVIEW TEST

The examination for which you applied requires an oral interview test. You have already taken the written test and you are now being called for the interview test – the final part of the formal examination.

You may think that it is not possible to prepare for an interview test and that there are no procedures to follow during an interview. Our purpose is to point out some things you can do in advance that will help you and some good rules to follow and pitfalls to avoid while you are being interviewed.

What is an interview supposed to test?

The written examination is designed to test the technical knowledge and competence of the candidate; the oral is designed to evaluate intangible qualities, not readily measured otherwise, and to establish a list showing the relative fitness of each candidate – as measured against his competitors – for the position sought. Scoring is not on the basis of "right" and "wrong," but on a sliding scale of values ranging from "not passable" to "outstanding." As a matter of fact, it is possible to achieve a relatively low score without a single "incorrect" answer because of evident weakness in the qualities being measured.

Occasionally, an examination may consist entirely of an oral test – either an individual or a group oral. In such cases, information is sought concerning the technical knowledges and abilities of the candidate, since there has been no written examination for this purpose. More commonly, however, an oral test is used to supplement a written examination.

Who conducts interviews?

The composition of oral boards varies among different jurisdictions. In nearly all, a representative of the personnel department serves as chairman. One of the members of the board may be a representative of the department in which the candidate would work. In some cases, "outside experts" are used, and, frequently, a businessman or some other representative of the general public is asked to serve. Labor and management or other special groups may be represented. The aim is to secure the services of experts in the appropriate field.

However the board is composed, it is a good idea (and not at all improper or unethical) to ascertain in advance of the interview who the members are and what groups they represent. When you are introduced to them, you will have some idea of their backgrounds and interests, and at least you will not stutter and stammer over their names.

What should be done before the interview?

While knowledge about the board members is useful and takes some of the surprise element out of the interview, there is other preparation which is more substantive. It *is* possible to prepare for an oral interview – in several ways:

1) Keep a copy of your application and review it carefully before the interview

This may be the only document before the oral board, and the starting point of the interview. Know what education and experience you have listed there, and the sequence and dates of all of it. Sometimes the board will ask you to review the highlights of your experience for them; you should not have to hem and haw doing it.

2) Study the class specification and the examination announcement

Usually, the oral board has one or both of these to guide them. The qualities, characteristics or knowledges required by the position sought are stated in these documents. They offer valuable clues as to the nature of the oral interview. For example, if the job involves supervisory responsibilities, the announcement will usually indicate that knowledge of modern supervisory methods and the qualifications of the candidate as a supervisor will be tested. If so, you can expect such questions, frequently in the form of a hypothetical situation which you are expected to solve. NEVER go into an oral without knowledge of the duties and responsibilities of the job you seek.

3) Think through each qualification required

Try to visualize the kind of questions you would ask if you were a board member. How well could you answer them? Try especially to appraise your own knowledge and background in each area, *measured against the job sought*, and identify any areas in which you are weak. Be critical and realistic – do not flatter yourself.

4) Do some general reading in areas in which you feel you may be weak

For example, if the job involves supervision and your past experience has NOT, some general reading in supervisory methods and practices, particularly in the field of human relations, might be useful. Do NOT study agency procedures or detailed manuals. The oral board will be testing your understanding and capacity, not your memory.

5) Get a good night's sleep and watch your general health and mental attitude

You will want a clear head at the interview. Take care of a cold or any other minor ailment, and of course, no hangovers.

What should be done on the day of the interview?

Now comes the day of the interview itself. Give yourself plenty of time to get there. Plan to arrive somewhat ahead of the scheduled time, particularly if your appointment is in the fore part of the day. If a previous candidate fails to appear, the board might be ready for you a bit early. By early afternoon an oral board is almost invariably behind schedule if there are many candidates, and you may have to wait. Take along a book or magazine to read, or your application to review, but leave any extraneous material in the waiting room when you go in for your interview. In any event, relax and compose yourself.

The matter of dress is important. The board is forming impressions about you – from your experience, your manners, your attitude, and your appearance. Give your personal appearance careful attention. Dress your best, but not your flashiest. Choose conservative, appropriate clothing, and be sure it is immaculate. This is a business interview, and your appearance should indicate that you regard it as such. Besides, being well groomed and properly dressed will help boost your confidence.

Sooner or later, someone will call your name and escort you into the interview room. *This is it.* From here on you are on your own. It is too late for any more preparation. But remember, you asked for this opportunity to prove your fitness, and you are here because your request was granted.

What happens when you go in?

The usual sequence of events will be as follows: The clerk (who is often the board stenographer) will introduce you to the chairman of the oral board, who will introduce you to the other members of the board. Acknowledge the introductions before you sit down. Do not be surprised if you find a microphone facing you or a stenotypist sitting by. Oral interviews are usually recorded in the event of an appeal or other review.

Usually the chairman of the board will open the interview by reviewing the highlights of your education and work experience from your application – primarily for the benefit of the other members of the board, as well as to get the material into the record. Do not interrupt or comment unless there is an error or significant misinterpretation; if that is the case, do not hesitate. But do not quibble about insignificant matters. Also, he will usually ask you some question about your education, experience or your present job – partly to get you to start talking and to establish the interviewing "rapport." He may start the actual questioning, or turn it over to one of the other members. Frequently, each member undertakes the questioning on a particular area, one in which he is perhaps most competent, so you can expect each member to participate in the examination. Because time is limited, you may also expect some rather abrupt switches in the direction the questioning takes, so do not be upset by it. Normally, a board member will not pursue a single line of questioning unless he discovers a particular strength or weakness.

After each member has participated, the chairman will usually ask whether any member has any further questions, then will ask you if you have anything you wish to add. Unless you are expecting this question, it may floor you. Worse, it may start you off on an extended, extemporaneous speech. The board is not usually seeking more information. The question is principally to offer you a last opportunity to present further qualifications or to indicate that you have nothing to add. So, if you feel that a significant qualification or characteristic has been overlooked, it is proper to point it out in a sentence or so. Do not compliment the board on the thoroughness of their examination – they have been sketchy, and you know it. If you wish, merely say, "No thank you, I have nothing further to add." This is a point where you can "talk yourself out" of a good impression or fail to present an important bit of information. Remember, *you close the interview yourself*.

The chairman will then say, "That is all, Mr. _____, thank you." Do not be startled; the interview is over, and quicker than you think. Thank him, gather your belongings and take your leave. Save your sigh of relief for the other side of the door.

How to put your best foot forward

Throughout this entire process, you may feel that the board individually and collectively is trying to pierce your defenses, seek out your hidden weaknesses and embarrass and confuse you. Actually, this is not true. They are obliged to make an appraisal of your qualifications for the job you are seeking, and they want to see you in your best light. Remember, they must interview all candidates and a non-cooperative candidate may become a failure in spite of their best efforts to bring out his qualifications. Here are 15 suggestions that will help you:

1) Be natural – Keep your attitude confident, not cocky

If you are not confident that you can do the job, do not expect the board to be. Do not apologize for your weaknesses, try to bring out your strong points. The board is interested in a positive, not negative, presentation. Cockiness will antagonize any board member and make him wonder if you are covering up a weakness by a false show of strength.

2) Get comfortable, but don't lounge or sprawl

Sit erectly but not stiffly. A careless posture may lead the board to conclude that you are careless in other things, or at least that you are not impressed by the importance of the occasion. Either conclusion is natural, even if incorrect. Do not fuss with your clothing, a pencil or an ashtray. Your hands may occasionally be useful to emphasize a point; do not let them become a point of distraction.

3) Do not wisecrack or make small talk

This is a serious situation, and your attitude should show that you consider it as such. Further, the time of the board is limited – they do not want to waste it, and neither should you.

4) Do not exaggerate your experience or abilities

In the first place, from information in the application or other interviews and sources, the board may know more about you than you think. Secondly, you probably will not get away with it. An experienced board is rather adept at spotting such a situation, so do not take the chance.

5) If you know a board member, do not make a point of it, yet do not hide it

Certainly you are not fooling him, and probably not the other members of the board. Do not try to take advantage of your acquaintanceship – it will probably do you little good.

6) Do not dominate the interview

Let the board do that. They will give you the clues – do not assume that you have to do all the talking. Realize that the board has a number of questions to ask you, and do not try to take up all the interview time by showing off your extensive knowledge of the answer to the first one.

7) Be attentive

You only have 20 minutes or so, and you should keep your attention at its sharpest throughout. When a member is addressing a problem or question to you, give him your undivided attention. Address your reply principally to him, but do not exclude the other board members.

8) Do not interrupt

A board member may be stating a problem for you to analyze. He will ask you a question when the time comes. Let him state the problem, and wait for the question.

9) Make sure you understand the question

Do not try to answer until you are sure what the question is. If it is not clear, restate it in your own words or ask the board member to clarify it for you. However, do not haggle about minor elements.

10) Reply promptly but not hastily

A common entry on oral board rating sheets is "candidate responded readily," or "candidate hesitated in replies." Respond as promptly and quickly as you can, but do not jump to a hasty, ill-considered answer.

11) Do not be peremptory in your answers

A brief answer is proper – but do not fire your answer back. That is a losing game from your point of view. The board member can probably ask questions much faster than you can answer them.

12) Do not try to create the answer you think the board member wants

He is interested in what kind of mind you have and how it works – not in playing games. Furthermore, he can usually spot this practice and will actually grade you down on it.

13) Do not switch sides in your reply merely to agree with a board member

Frequently, a member will take a contrary position merely to draw you out and to see if you are willing and able to defend your point of view. Do not start a debate, yet do not surrender a good position. If a position is worth taking, it is worth defending.

14) Do not be afraid to admit an error in judgment if you are shown to be wrong

The board knows that you are forced to reply without any opportunity for careful consideration. Your answer may be demonstrably wrong. If so, admit it and get on with the interview.

15) Do not dwell at length on your present job

The opening question may relate to your present assignment. Answer the question but do not go into an extended discussion. You are being examined for a *new* job, not your present one. As a matter of fact, try to phrase ALL your answers in terms of the job for which you are being examined.

Basis of Rating

Probably you will forget most of these "do's" and "don'ts" when you walk into the oral interview room. Even remembering them all will not ensure you a passing grade. Perhaps you did not have the qualifications in the first place. But remembering them will help you to put your best foot forward, without treading on the toes of the board members.

Rumor and popular opinion to the contrary notwithstanding, an oral board wants you to make the best appearance possible. They know you are under pressure – but they also want to see how you respond to it as a guide to what your reaction would be under the pressures of the job you seek. They will be influenced by the degree of poise you display, the personal traits you show and the manner in which you respond.

ABOUT THIS BOOK

This book contains tests divided into Examination Sections. Go through each test, answering every question in the margin. We have also attached a sample answer sheet at the back of the book that can be removed and used. At the end of each test look at the answer key and check your answers. On the ones you got wrong, look at the right answer choice and learn. Do not fill in the answers first. Do not memorize the questions and answers, but understand the answer and principles involved. On your test, the questions will likely be different from the samples. Questions are changed and new ones added. If you understand these past questions you should have success with any changes that arise. Tests may consist of several types of questions. We have additional books on each subject should more study be advisable or necessary for you. Finally, the more you study, the better prepared you will be. This book is intended to be the last thing you study before you walk into the examination room. Prior study of relevant texts is also recommended. NLC publishes some of these in our Fundamental Series. Knowledge and good sense are important factors in passing your exam. Good luck also helps. So now study this Passbook, absorb the material contained within and take that knowledge into the examination. Then do your best to pass that exam.

EXAMINATION SECTION

EXAMINATION SECTION
TEST 1

DIRECTIONS: Each question or incomplete statement is followed by several suggested, answers or completions. Select the one that BEST answers the question or completes the statement. *PRINT THE LETTER OF THE CORRECT ANSWER IN THE SPACE AT THE RIGHT.*

1. The authority to establish zoning ordinances by a community comes from

    A. the police power of the state
    B. local determination
    C. the federal government
    D. implied powers of the community

2. On a land use map, the standard color used to designate residential use is

    A. green   B. blue   C. purple   D. yellow

3. In population analysis, a population pyramid indicates

    A. male and female age groupings
    B. total population projections
    C. fertility ratios
    D. educational achievements

4. The determination of a standard metropolitan statistical area is established by

    A. local considerations   B. regional agencies
    C. the U.S. Census Bureau   D. state agencies

5. The population census of the United States is taken every _____ years.

    A. 2   B. 4   C. 5   D. 10

6. There are strong indications that planning agencies are developing a new approach to the traditional methods of city planning.
   This new approach is called

    A. advocacy planning
    B. long-range physical planning
    C. community development
    D. policies planning

7. A key element of a comprehensive plan for a community is the

    A. zoning ordinance   B. land use plan
    C. official map   D. subdivision regulation

8. The official map of a community is a document that

    A. shows population projections and educational trends
    B. pinpoints the location of future streets and other public facilities
    C. identifies capital improvements and budgets
    D. indicates all community facilities

9. During the past decade, planning programs generally have become increasingly concerned with which one of the following?

   A. Long-range physical design
   B. Highway locations
   C. Social welfare
   D. Natural resources

10. The city planning process encompasses several basic phases. Which one of the following phases would NOT be considered typical?

    A. Cost-benefit analysis
    B. Goal formulation
    C. Data collection and research
    D. Plan preparation and programming

11. The MOST common use of easements in new housing subdivisions is for

    A. air rights   B. utilities
    C. open space   D. absorption fields

12. The phrase *non-complying use* relates to which one of the following regulations?

    A. Zoning Ordinance   B. Building Code
    C. Subdivision regulations D. Health Code

13. Performance standards are generally associated with which one of the following types of zoning districts?

    A. Residential   B. Commercial
    C. Manufacturing   D. Flood plain

14. The PRIMARY goal of cluster-type development is to

    A. increase population density
    B. insure open space
    C. discourage rapid development
    D. bypass zoning requirements

15. Which of the following is MOST closely related to the land-use intensity standards developed by the Federal Housing Administration?

    A. Quality of housing   B. Planned unit development
    C. Low-cost housing   D. Land management policy

16. If the density of a residential subdivision is 8 dwelling units per acre, then the average size lot should be APPROXIMATELY

    A. 25 ft. x 100 ft.   B. 55 ft. x 100 ft.
    C. 100 ft. x 100 ft.   D. 200 ft. x 200 ft.

17. In planning the open parking area for community facilities, the amount of space allocated per care should be APPROXIMATELY _____ sq.ft.

    A. 150   B. 300   C. 600   D. 800

18. Which of the following facilities would be MOST appropriate on the roof of a building? 18.____

    A. Stolport B. Heliport
    C. Airport   D. Cargo port

19. Sanitary landfill is a method of 19.____

    A. sewage disposal B. composting
    C. incineration   D. refuse disposal

20. Which of the following is NOT considered to be an air pollutant by the Environmental Protection Agency? 20.____

    A. Nitrates   B. Sulfur oxides
    C. Carbon monoxide   D. Hydrocarbons

21. Which of the following recreation facilities is NOT considered a typical neighborhood facility? 21.____

    A. Tot lot   B. Playground
    C. Wading pool   D. Playfield

22. Which of the following methods would be the MOST accurate in making a population projection for a small community? 22.____

    A. Migration and natural increase
    B. Apportionment and voting records
    C. School enrollment and housing starts
    D. Geometric extrapolation

23. When a planning map is to be reproduced to different sizes, the map scale should be expressed 23.____

    A. mathematically   B. in graphic form
    C. in feet and inches D. by metes and bounds

24. The one of the following characteristics which is NOT typical of new industrial parks is 24.____

    A. off-street loading B. extensive landscaping
    C. employee parking   D. 2-story structures

25. A greenbelt surrounding a community can be used for many activities.
    The one of the following activities LEAST appropriate for greenbelt use is 25.____

    A. farming   B. recreation
    C. local shopping D. flood plain control

KEY (CORRECT ANSWERS)

1. A
2. D
3. A
4. C
5. D

6. D
7. B
8. B
9. C
10. A

11. B
12. A
13. C
14. B
15. B

16. B
17. B
18. B
19. D
20. A

21. D
22. A
23. B
24. D
25. C

TEST 2

DIRECTIONS: Each question or incomplete statement is followed by several suggested answers or completions. Select the one that BEST answers the question or completes the statement. *PRINT THE LETTER OF THE CORRECT ANSWER IN THE SPACE AT THE RIGHT.*

1. The *neighborhood unit* concept does NOT provide for 1.____
   A. elementary schools B. playgrounds
   C. local shopping D. industrial development

2. Which of the following areas is LEAST likely to be considered part of social welfare planning? 2.____
   A. Urban design B. Education
   C. Health D. Anti-poverty

3. Both the census of business and the census of manufacturing compiled by the U.S. Bureau of the Census are made every _____ years. 3.____
   A. three B. five C. seven D. ten

4. The MOST frequently used governmental source for topographical maps is the U.S. 4.____
   A. Department of Agriculture
   B. Geological Survey
   C. Department of Housing and Urban Development
   D. Coast Guard

5. The importance of assessed valuation of land and buildings to a community is to 5.____
   A. establish school taxes
   B. establish property taxes
   C. determine tax exemptions
   D. determine land uses

6. Of the following countries, the MOST extensive progress in establishing new towns during the 20th century has taken place in 6.____
   A. the United States B. France
   C. Italy D. England

7. A street classification system is PRIMARILY used for street 7.____
   A. naming B. construction
   C. differentiation D. location

8. The *Greenbelt* towns were a product of the 8.____
   A. city beautiful movement
   B. garden city movement
   C. atomic energy commission
   D. resettlement administration

9. The apportionment method of population projection is concerned PRIMARILY with

   A. migration
   B. natural increase
   C. large geographic areas
   D. birth rate

10. Under ideal conditions, which type of parking arrangement should yield the MOST parking spaces?

    A. Parallel
    B. 45°
    C. 60°
    D. 90°

11. A MAJOR disadvantage of a depressed highway through a built-up area as compared to a highway on grade is its

    A. poor appearance
    B. inadequate width of right-of-way
    C. lack of access
    D. noise generation

12. The customary test made to determine the ability of a soil to drain off liquids, such as those discharged by a cesspool, is known as the _____ test.

    A. percolation
    B. absorption
    C. drainage
    D. sump

13. The Mitchell-Lama Housing Law was originally intended to assist the construction of

    A. low-income housing
    B. middle-income housing
    C. suburban residential projects
    D. housing for mixed racial communities

14. A community will MOST frequently acquire the development rights of existing farm land in order to

    A. protect land values
    B. provide sites for public projects
    C. insure open space
    D. develop a land bank

15. In recent years, local participation in the city planning process has *substantially* increased because of the

    A. establishment of local school boards
    B. high crime rate in the streets
    C. emergence of private citizen organizations
    D. establishment of community planning boards

16. A unique feature of the State Urban Development Corporation when first established was that it

    A. was an autonomous organization
    B. was not required to conform to local zoning regulations
    C. could only build housing when invited by local communities
    D. used only private funds for its projects

17. The concept of *defensible space* has recently emerged to help fight crime in urban areas. The principle of *defensible space* is that public areas should be

    A. completely enclosed
    B. eliminated
    C. placed adjacent to areas of activity
    D. patroled by volunteer citizen groups

18. Of the following, the MAJOR planning implication of a 3-bedroom dwelling unit as compared to a 1-bedroom dwelling unit is that

    A. the family with the larger dwelling unit has more income
    B. with larger dwelling units there will be fewer municipal services necessary
    C. more children will be enrolled in school
    D. smaller dwelling units are cheaper to build than larger units

19. A landscaped buffer strip is MOST appropriately placed between which of the following land uses?

    A. Light and heavy manufacturing
    B. Residential and commercial
    C. Commercial and manufacturing
    D. Residential of low density and residential of high density

20. The employment trend in the city over the past 20 years has shown that

    A. *both* white collar and blue collar jobs have increased
    B. *both* white collar and blue collar jobs have decreased
    C. *only* white collar jobs have decreased
    D. *only* blue collar jobs have decreased

21. For traffic safety, the BEST angle between two intersecting streets is

    A. 15   B. 30   C. 45   D. 90

22. In the city, the system used by the tax department to identify property is by

    A. house numbers   B. zoning maps
    C. block and lot numbers   D. the official city map

23. The name of the report by which the U.S. Environmental Protection Agency establishes the effect of a proposed project on the environment is called the

    A. input-output analysis   B. economic base study
    C. ambient air study   D. impact statement

24. Planners recommend that utility lines be located underground because utility lines built this way are

    A. cheaper to construct
    B. not required to follow street alignments
    C. aesthetically more attractive
    D. more efficient

25. *Scatter-site* housing means that the housing will be 25._____
    A. located in all use districts
    B. built with large areas of recreation space between buildings
    C. of different heights on each site
    D. built on small, by-passed sites in built-up areas

KEY (CORRECT ANSWERS)

1. D
2. A
3. B
4. B
5. B

6. D
7. C
8. D
9. C
10. D

11. C
12. A
13. B
14. C
15. D

16. B
17. C
18. C
19. B
20. D

21. D
22. C
23. D
24. C
25. D

EXAMINATION SECTION
TEST 1

DIRECTIONS: Each question or incomplete statement is followed by several suggested answers or completions. Select the one that BEST answers the question or completes the Statement. *PRINT THE LETTER OF THE CORRECT ANSWER IN THE SPACE AT THE RIGHT.*

1. City planning should aim at

    A. over-all planning
    B. administrative planning
    C. planning of only physical facilities
    D. planning of resources

    1.____

2. The director of planning of a local planning agency is *usually* responsible to the

    A. planning commission   B. city council
    C. mayor   D. city manager

    2.____

3. The official map is subject to change ONLY by the

    A. planning commission   B. city engineer
    C. legislative body   D. mayor

    3.____

4. An official map of a city is generally adopted by, and can ONLY be changed by action of the

    A. city engineer   B. planning board
    C. legislative body   D. zoning board of appeals

    4.____

5. Zoning regulations are generally administered by the

    A. building department   B. planning commission
    C. zoning board of appeals   D. planning director

    5.____

6. Logical extent of area which should be included in basic studies for a comprehensive city plan is

    A. entire residential area
    B. the neighborhood
    C. area bounded by city boundaries
    D. urban region

    6.____

7. The safest angle (in degrees) for the intersection of two local streets is

    A. 45   B. 60   C. 90   D. 120

    7.____

8. The city-beautiful movement is *usually* associated with work of

    A. L'Enfant   B. Burnham   C. Wright   D. Howard

    8.____

9. The garden city movement is *usually* associated with

    A. Adams   B. Moses   C. Dahir   D. Howard

    9.____

10. The power to permit variances to the zoning resolution is *usually* vested in the 10.____

   A. City Planning Commission
   B. Building Department
   C. City Council
   D. Board of Standards and Appeals

11. "Multiple Dwelling Law" is a 11.____

   A. federal law
   B. state law
   C. municipal ordinance
   D. law to protect landlords and hotels

12. The BEST map to use in planning a street layout for a new development is 12.____

   A. topographic   B. planimetric
   C. photo-mosaic   D. hydrographic chart

13. MAXIMUM auto traffic carrying capacity of a city street is attained at approximate speed 13.____
    of _____ M.P.H.

   A. 10-15   B. 15-25   C. 25-40   D. 40-55

14. A decelerating lane would *most likely* be used in conjunction with a 14.____

   A. bridge approach
   B. highway exit
   C. sharp curve on a highway
   D. steep grade on a highway

15. Use of curved streets in suburban development is *desirable* because it 15.____

   A. increases sight-distance for motorists
   B. makes a lot layout simpler
   C. forces motorists to reduce speed
   D. reduces surveying costs

16. The LEAST important requirement for a fire hydrant is 16.____

   A. accessibility   B. artistic design
   C. frost proof   D. mechanical reliability

17. In general, the *highest* tax return per acre of developed land is 17.____

   A. business   B. industry
   C. apartments   D. single family homes

18. The percentage of developed land area in a city normally taken up by the street system 18.____
    is about _____ %.

   A. 15   B. 25   C. 35   D. 45

19. The greatest amount of land in Manhattan is used for 19.____

   A. residences   B. stores
   C. offices   D. industry

20. The three "Greenbelt" towns in the United States after World War II were built by   20._____
    A. private capital
    B. the F.H.A.
    C. the Resettlement Administration
    D. the Department of Agriculture

KEY (CORRECT ANSWERS)

1.	A	11.	B
2.	A	12.	A
3.	C	13.	B
4.	C	14.	B
5.	A	15.	C
6.	D	16.	B
7.	C	17.	A
8.	B	18.	C
9.	D	19.	A
10.	D	20.	C

TEST 2

DIRECTIONS: Each question consists of a statement. You are to indicate whether the statement is TRUE (T) or FALSE (F). *PRINT THE LETTER OF THE CORRECT ANSWER IN THE SPACE AT THE RIGHT.*

1. In an *ideal plan,* radial express highways should lead to and through the downtown business center of a city.   1.____

2. In an ideal city plan for a large city, there should be circumferential transit lines NOT giving direct service to the central business district.   2.____

3. Modern limited access express highways for mixed traffic may appropriately be estimated, for purposes of adequacy of design, to have a practical capacity of 1200 to 1500 vehicles per lane per hour.   3.____

4. A city that is growing by constant decennial increments of total population would have a *straight-line* population curve when plotted on semi-logarithmic cross-section paper.   4.____

5. An infant mortality rate of 60 per 1000 live births per annum is representative of good health conditions in northeastern cities of the U.S.   5.____

6. A city which has 4 acres of land in use by industry, per 100 total resident population, would be considered highly industrialized.   6.____

7. The federal government, through the Department of Transportation, assists in financing new state highways within and outside corporate limits of cities.   7.____

8. The "riding habit" of Los Angeles would be expected to be *greater than* that of New York because of greater relative extent of use of private automobiles.   8.____

9. Because of lane friction and traffic weaving, a 4-lane one-way express roadway will NOT achieve a greater vehicle discharge per hour than a 3-lane one-way express roadway, all other design features being the same.   9.____

10. It is *good* practice to locate future playgrounds NOT more than one-quarter mile from any part of residential areas to be served.   10.____

11. An efficiently laid-out 18-hole golf course, under average topographic conditions, can be accomodated within 110 acres.   11.____

12. Elementary school sites of at least 5 acres are representative of good practice.   12.____

13. Senior high school sites of 25 to 40 acres are NOT considered extravagant or excessive under modern design standards.   13.____

14. Future school enrollments can be estimated by extrapolation of a curve showing percentage of total population which was enrolled in the school system in past years.   14.____

15. A "neighborhood unit" is a term used to embrace those planned residential area which constitute area of service of 1 junior high school.   15.____

16. "Company housing" is customarily used to describe colonies of dwelling units owned by an industrial corporation and rented individually to its employees.   16.____

17. In a *well-designed* residential subdivision, area of land in streets should NOT exceed 20 per cent of total area. 17.____

18. It is accepted *good* zoning practice to require large parking areas be screened from adjacent residential zones by landscaping. 18.____

19. "Floor area ratio" is quotient of ground floor area of a building divided by area of its lot. 19.____

20. The term "Unrestricted Districts" designates districts for which no use or area regulations or restrictions are provided by present zoning resolutions. 20.____

21. A rectangular block 200' x 810' has an area of about four acres. 21.____

22. Capacity of a highway *increases* directly with the speed. 22.____

23. A truck farm is prohibited in a residential district. 23.____

24. On a street with a crowned pavement, grade may be reduced to 0.0%. 24.____

25. Climate has NO effect on design of combined sewers. 25.____

26. Subgrade of a highway is the *lowest* grade ensuring adequate drainage. 26.____

27. Underdrainage results when inadequate storm sewers are provided. 27.____

28. Plans for bridges over navigable waterways require Army Corps of Engineers approval. 28.____

29. On a street with crossings at grade, the ONLY safety features added by widening a narrow median strip are further separation of opposing lanes of traffic and reduction of headlight glare. 29.____

30. In rural areas, need of sidewalks along highways depends on density of vehicular and pedestrian traffic and design speed of highway. 30.____

31. It is standard practice to design 2-lane highways with minimum sight distance such that overtaking and passing is possible in any section of the highway. 31.____

32. Widening pavements on curves is for *psychological* reasons ONLY. 32.____

33. An advantage of a concrete pavement is its high salvage value. 33.____

34. A *large* part of city planning consists of correction of mistakes. 34.____

35. Distribution of population is *usually* shown on a dot or density map. 35.____

36. A series of density maps showing population distribution at various dates is of NO more value to a city planner than the latest map of series. 36.____

37. In a *free* port, goods may be stored, repacked, manufactured, and reexported WITHOUT customs formalities. 37.____

38. Urban blight is due *solely* to lack of planning in original development. 38.____

39. The Chamber of Commerce of the United States recommends municipalities adopt building codes permitting use of any material or method of construction which meets minimum required standards of performance. 39.____

40. An accepted reliable method of estimating future population of small municipalities (under 10,000), for 5 years forward from the last census, involves extending past trend of birth rates, death rates, annual statistics of new dwelling units constructed, old dwelling units demolished, and average size of family. 40.____

KEY (CORRECT ANSWERS)

1. F	11. T	21. T	31. F
2. T	12. T	22. F	32. F
3. T	13. T	23. F	33. T
4. F	14. F	24. F	34. T
5. F	15. F	25. F	35. T
6. T	16. T	26. F	36. F
7. T	17. T	27. F	37. T
8. F	18. T	28. T	38. F
9. F	19. F	29. F	39. T
10. T	20. F	30. T	40. T

EXAMINATION SECTION
TEST 1

DIRECTIONS: Each question or incomplete statement is followed by several suggested answers or completions. Select the one that BEST answers the question or completes the statement. *PRINT THE LETTER OF THE CORRECT ANSWER IN THE SPACE AT THE RIGHT.*

Questions 1-5.

DIRECTIONS: Questions 1 through 5 are based on the table shown below.

POPULATION, URBAN AND RURAL, BY RACE: 2000 TO 2020

In thousands, except percent. An urbanized area comprises at least 1 city of 50,000 inhabitants (central city) plus contiguous, closely settled areas (urban fringe). Data for 2000 and 2010 according to urban definition used in the 2010 census; 2020 data according to the 2020 definition.

YEAR AND AREA	TOTAL	WHITE	ALL OTHER	PERCENT DISTRIBUTION		
				TOTAL	WHITE	ALL OTHER
2000, total population	151,326	135,150	16,176	100.0	100.0	100.0
Urban	96,847	86,864	9,983	64.0	64.3	61.7
Inside urbanized areas	69,249	61,925	7,324	45.8	45.8	45.3
Central cities	48,377	42,042	6,335	32.0	31.1	39.2
Urban fringe	20,872	19,883	989	13.8	14.7	6.1
Outside urbanized areas	27,598	24,939	2,659	18.2	18.5	16.4
Rural	54,479	48,286	6,193	36.0	35.7	38.3
2010, total population	179,323	158,832	20,491	100.0	100.0	100.0
Urban	125,269	110,428	14,840	69.9	69.5	72.4
Inside urbanized areas	95,848	83,770	12,079	53.5	52.7	58.9
Central cities	57,975	47,627	10,348	32.3	30.0	50.5
Urban fringe	37,873	36,143	1,371	21.1	22.8	8.4
Outside urbanized areas	29,420	26,658	2,762	16.4	16.8	13.5
Rural	54,054	48,403	5,651	30.1	30.5	27.6
2020, total population	203,212	177,749	25,463	100.0	100.0	100.0
Urban	149,325	128,773	20,552	73.5	72.4	80.7
Inside urbanized areas	118,447	100,952	17,495	58.3	56.8	68.7
Central cities	63,922	49,547	14,375	31.5	27.9	56.5
Urban fringe	54,525	51,405	3,120	26.8	28.9	12.3
Outside urbanized areas	30,878	27,822	3,057	15.2	15.7	12.0
Rural	53,887	48,976	4,911	26.5	27.6	19.3

1. The ratio of urban to rural population in 2000 was MOST NEARLY

    A. 3:1   B. 4:1   C. 2:1   D. 14:1

2. According to the table, the trend of population inside urban areas has been

    A. towards greater concentration
    B. towards less concentration
    C. towards stabilization
    D. erratic

3. Since 2000, the urban fringe white population has substantially increased while the urban fringe other population has

   A. slightly decreased
   B. greatly decreased
   C. remained the same
   D. increased moderately

   3.____

4. Over the years, the percentage of the urban white population as compared with the percentage of the total urban population has

   A. remained relatively constant
   B. substantially decreased
   C. substantially increased
   D. varied

   4.____

5. Select the one of the following which BEST describes the central city white population rate of decrease since 2000 as compared with the central city black population rate of increase.

   A. The central city white population rate of decrease has been greater than the central city black population rate of increase.
   B. The central city white and black populations have not increased to a significant degree.
   C. The central city white population rate of decrease has been equal to the central city black population rate of increase.
   D. The central city white population rate of decrease has been less than the central city black population rate of increase.

   5.____

Questions 6-10.

DIRECTIONS: Questions 6 through 10 are to be answered on the basis of the table shown below.

STANDARDS FOR RECREATION AREAS

TYPE OF AREA	ACRES PER 1,000 POPULATION	SIZE OF SITE (ACRES) IDEAL	SIZE OF SITE (ACRES) MINIMUM	RADIUS OF AREA SERVED (MILES)
Playgrounds	1.5	4	2	0.5
Neighborhood parks	2.0	10	5	0.5
Playfields	1.5	15	10	1.5
Community parks	3.5	100	40	2.0
District parks	2.0	200	100	3.0
Regional parks and reservations	15.0	500-1,000	varies	10.0

6. What is the MINIMUM number of playfields that a community of 15,000 people may contain if the size of each is kept within the limits shown in the table?

   A. 4   B. 10   C. 6   D. 2

   6.____

7. If, as far as possible, ideal sized playgrounds are built, how many IDEAL SIZED playgrounds should a community of 12,000 people contain?

   A. 4   B. 8   C. 1   D. 10

   7.____

8. Approximately how many people can a community park of 200 acres serve? 8._____

   A. 120,000   B. 80,000   C. 55,000   D. 20,000

9. If only minimum sized neighborhood parks are built, how many will be required for a population of 20,000? 9._____

   A. 5   B. 2   C. 8   D. 12

10. A community of 75,000 persons is evenly distributed over a 5 square mile area. Of the following, the number and size of playgrounds that would BEST satisfy the standards is _____ playgrounds @ _____ acres each. 10._____

    A. 5; 7.5   B. 35; 3.5   C. 10; 10   D. 50; 1.5

11. The illustration shown at the right is an example of a 11._____

    A. simple grade separation
    B. simple interchange of a freeway with a highway
    C. three-level interchange
    D. T interchange

12. The practical MINIMUM number of cars per hour that can be carried per lane on a limited access roadway with uninterrupted flow is considered to be APPROXIMATELY 12._____

    A. 750   B. 1,500   C. 5,000   D. 10,000

13. A street that is open at only one end, with provision for a turn-around at the other, is called a 13._____

    A. local street   B. cul-de-sac
    C. loop street   D. minor street

14. Which of the following shopping center types is the local source of staple goods and daily services? 14._____

    A. Central Business District
    B. Regional Shopping Center
    C. Highway Strip Development
    D. Neighborhood Shopping Center

15. *Air rights* refers to the concept that 15._____

    A. all people are entitled to clean air
    B. vistas from apartments cannot be obstructed
    C. buildings can be constructed over railroads or highways
    D. buildings should be oriented towards the prevailing breezes

16. The one of the following LEAST likely to be considered an integral part of urban design is 16._____

    A. spatial forms   B. surfaces
    C. vistas   D. underground utilities

Questions 17-21.

DIRECTIONS: Questions 17 through 21 are based upon the table shown below.

LIVE BIRTHS, DEATHS, MARRIAGES, AND DIVORCES: 1940-1991

YEAR	Number (1,000)					Rate per 1,000 Population				
	BIRTHS	DEATHS TOTAL	DEATHS INFANT	MAR- RIAGES	DIVOR- CES	BIRTHS	DEATHS TOTAL	DEATHS INFANT	MAR- RIAGES	DIVOR- CES
1940	2,777	697	(NA)	948	83	30.1	14.7	(NA)	10.3	0.9
1945	2,965	816	78	1,008	104	29.5	13.2	99.9	10.0	1.0
1950	2,950	1,118	130	1,274	171	27.7	13.0	85.8	12.0	1.6
1955	2,909	1,192	135	1,188	175	25.1	11.7	71.7	10.3	1.5
1960	2,618	1,327	142	1,127	196	21.3	11.3	64.6	9.2	1.6
1965	2,377	1,393	120	1,327	218	18.7	10.9	55.7	10.4	1.7
1970	2,559	1,417	111	1,596	264	19.4	10.8	47.0	12.1	2.0
1975	2,858	1,402	105	1,613	485	20.4	10.6	38.3	12.2	3.5
1980	3,632	1,452	104	1,667	385	24.1	9.6	29.2	11.1	2.6
1985	4,104	1,529	107	1,531	377	25.0	9.3	26.4	9.3	2.3
1990	4,258	1,712	111	1,523	393	23.7	9.5	26.0	8.5	2.2
1991	4,268	1,702	108	1,548	414	23.3	9.3	25.3	8.5	2.3

NA   Not Available

17. From 1940 to 1991, the birth rate has

   A. approximately doubled
   B. remained stable
   C. been reduced by 25%
   D. had two breaks in its downward progression

18. A comparison of the total population death rate to the infant death rate shows that

   A. the two rates have remained constant
   B. the infant death rate is greater
   C. the total population death rate has decreased at a faster rate
   D. infants had a greater chance to survive in 1965 than in 1980

19. In 1945, about one marriage out of 10 ended in divorce.
    In which of the following years would the rate be LESS?

   A. 1985   B. 1965   C. 1950   D. 1940

20. The significance of the decrease in the infant death rate is that

   A. family size will increase
   B. family size will decrease
   C. family size will not be affected
   D. children will become a smaller percentage of the total population

21. According to the chart, the total death rate declined from 14.7 in 1940 to 9.3 in 1991, yet each year more people have died. This fact is MOST likely accounted for by

   A. poor reporting techniques
   B. the decrease in the mortality rate
   C. the increase of total population
   D. the increase of older people in the total population

22. The type of interchange pictured in the illustration shown at the right is called a _____ interchange.

    A. simple
    B. cloverleaf
    C. universal
    D. Bel Geddes

23. This type of interchange (pictured in the preceding question) is used when

    A. topographic conditions are difficult
    B. traffic volumes are heavy
    C. a major and minor road intersect
    D. two major roads intersect

24. The one of the following basic requirements which would NOT be considered an integral part of a comprehensive plan is

    A. a capital improvement program
    B. physical design proposals
    C. long-range policy statements
    D. social and economic considerations

Questions 25-28.

DIRECTIONS: Questions 25 through 28 are based on the data shown below, which indicates total housing units.

HOUSING UNITS: 1960 to 1990
NUMBER IN THOUSANDS

| □□□ TOTAL | ≡ INSIDE SMSA'S | ☐ IN CENTRAL CITIES |

(SMSA's = Standard Metropolitan Statistical Areas)

1990
- Total: 68,679
- Inside SMSA's: 46,295
- In Central Cities: 22,594

1980
- Total: 58,326
- Inside SMSA's: 36,386
- In Central Cities: 19,622

1970
- Total: 45,983
- Inside SMSA's: 25,626
- In Central Cities: 15,120

1960
- Total: 37,326

25. The period of GREATEST production of housing units was

   A. 1950-60   B. 1980-90   C. 1970-80   D. 1960-70

26. The location of the LARGEST gains in housing units since 1960 was in the

   A. suburban areas   B. central cities
   C. SMSA's   D. rural areas

27. Contrary to many misconceptions, the above data shows that the central cities are

   A. losing population to the suburbs
   B. keeping pace with the overall housing development
   C. showing strong development trends
   D. growing, but at a decreasing rate

28. Based on the above data, which of the following statements is MOST accurate?

    A. The housing stock is rapidly becoming outdated.
    B. More new homes are located in suburban areas than in central cities.
    C. The housing supply is rapidly catching up to the demand.
    D. The majority of the population is located in the SMSA's.

29. The name of the long-range schedule of major projects and their estimated costs over a period of 5-10 years is the

    A. budget
    B. comprehensive plan
    C. capital improvement program
    D. input-output program

30. *Cost Benefit Analysis* is a method used to

    A. determine budget compliance
    B. compare costs and benefits of a particular investment
    C. evaluate productivity in school construction
    D. establish social benefits for a neighborhood

31. A *workable program* is a SIGNIFICANT element of a(n)

    A. urban renewal program
    B. comprehensive plan
    C. capital improvement program
    D. urban design program

32. Which of the following would NOT be considered a major type of municipal planning agency in the United States?

    A. An independent planning commission
    B. The planning department
    C. A community development department
    D. A local renewal agency

33. Townhouses are MOST closely related to which of the following types of residential construction?

    A. Garden apartments
    B. Row houses
    C. High-rise complexes
    D. Semi-attached houses

34. The one of the following which could NOT be considered an accessory use in a residence district is a

    A. garage
    B. greenhouse
    C. dwelling
    D. storage shed

35. The ratio of parking space to retail floor area in a major regional shopping center would MOST often be

    A. 1:1   B. 3:1   C. 6:1   D. 10:1

KEY (CORRECT ANSWERS)

1.	C	16.	D
2.	A	17.	C
3.	D	18.	B
4.	A	19.	D
5.	D	20.	C
6.	D	21.	C
7.	A	22.	B
8.	C	23.	D
9.	C	24.	A
10.	B	25.	C
11.	A	26.	A
12.	B	27.	D
13.	B	28.	B
14.	D	29.	C
15.	C	30.	B
31.	A		
32.	D		
33.	B		
34.	C		
35.	B		

TEST 2

DIRECTIONS: Each question or incomplete statement is followed by several suggested answers or completions. Select the one that BEST answers the question or completes the statement. *PRINT THE LETTER OF THE CORRECT ANSWER IN THE SPACE AT THE RIGHT.*

1. When the term *density* is commonly employed as a measure of land use, it refers to the   1.____

    A. number of persons   B. land coverage
    C. number of buildings   D. number of dwelling units

2. The *City Beautiful* movement was an outgrowth of the   2.____

    A. Bauhaus School in 1920
    B. Chicago World's Fair in 1893
    C. N.Y.C. Zoning Ordinance of 1916
    D. planning concepts of Emilio Sitte

3. The American Greenbelt towns were built to   3.____

    A. create open space
    B. establish independent satellite communities
    C. establish residential *dormitory* communities
    D. disperse urban population

4. The FIRST United States Housing Act was passed by Congress in   4.____

    A. 1929   B. 1949   C. 1941   D. 1937

5. A specific ratio of permissible floor space to lot area is known as   5.____

    A. floor area ratio   B. open space ratio
    C. sky exposure plane   D. lot coverage

6. A *protective covenant* can BEST be described as a(n)   6.____

    A. zoning ordinance   B. easement
    C. fire insurance policy   D. deed restriction

7. Underground utility lines are PREFERRED by most planners rather than overhead lines because underground lines   7.____

    A. are more accessible for maintenance
    B. cost less
    C. are not visible
    D. are laid in proper easements

8. If a local street right-of-way is 50 feet, the paved width of the street is GENERALLY _____ feet.   8.____

    A. 18   B. 26   C. 44   D. 50

9. The term *zero population growth* refers to the concept that

   A. the population will eventually become extinct
   B. married couples will not bear children
   C. each family will produce only two children
   D. parents will be subject to a planned schedule of parenthood

10. The MOST common dimensions of a half-acre residential lot are

    A. 100 ft. x 100 ft.
    B. 100 ft. x 200 ft.
    C. 120 ft. x 150 ft.
    D. 200 ft. x 200 ft.

11. As a general rule, large street trees should be planted

    A. 25 feet apart
    B. 50-75 feet apart
    C. 150-200 feet apart
    D. spaced randomly

12. A key regulation of a zoning ordinance relates to the

    A. architectural style of a building
    B. slope of a site
    C. height and bulk of buildings
    D. subsoil conditions

13. Under which one of the following authorities are zoning ordinances adopted by local communities?

    A. Police power
    B. Community power
    C. Will of the people
    D. Common law

14. MOST state enabling laws require that zoning regulations be based upon a

    A. land use plan
    B. base map
    C. comprehensive plan
    D. topographical map

15. The OBJECTIVE of an *interim zoning ordinance* is to

    A. zone only a portion of the community for a special purpose
    B. maintain existing conditions until a more comprehensive ordinance is prepared
    C. create a special district
    D. allow greater freedom in interpretation and utilization of the zoning regulations

16. A *non-conforming* use is

    A. a use which requires special approval to remain
    B. a building that does not comply with yard or bulk regulations
    C. one that is not permitted in a specific district
    D. a building which is structurally unsafe

17. A variance is granted by a board of appeals to

    A. obtain financial relief
    B. provide a balance of power
    C. test community opinion
    D. relieve practical difficulty and hardship

18. Which of the following zoning regulations, taken by itself, would permit the MOST floor area of building on a specific lot?
A

    A. floor area ratio of 3:1
    B. maximum lot coverage of 60%
    C. maximum building height of 50 feet
    D. parking ratio of 2:1

19. Sewers used to carry rain or surface water to a body of water so as to prevent flooding are called _____ sewers.

    A. sanitary   B. storm   C. combined   D. overflow

20. The *Garden City* concept was made famous through a book written by

    A. Sir Patrick Abercombie   B. Patrick Geddes
    C. Ebenezer Howard   D. Sir Raymond Unwin

21. *Broadacre City* was advocated as a concept of urban development by

    A. F.L. Wright   B. Corbusier
    C. Saarinen   D. Geddes

22. The man who can BEST be associated with the planning principle of *high density-low coverage* is

    A. Wright   B. VanderRohe
    C. Saarinen   D. Corbusier

23. The AVERAGE number of persons per household in the United States in 1970 was MOST NEARLY

    A. 2.0   B. 2.5   C. 3.0   D. 3.5

24. Which of the following methods would be the MOST accurate in making population projections?

    A. Migration and natural increase
    B. Apportionment
    C. School enrollment
    D. Geometric extrapolation

25. According to the 1990 census, the total population of the United States was MOST NEARLY _____ million persons.

    A. 190   B. 200   C. 280   D. 350

26. After the amounts of different land uses in a medium-size city have been tabulated, which of the following percentages of the total developed land would USUALLY be utilized for streets?

    A. 12%   B. 20%   C. 30%   D. 8%

27. During the past twenty years, the MOST significant factor causing reorientation of traditional urban land use patterns has been

    A. express highway construction
    B. airport development
    C. new schools
    D. permissive zoning ordinances

28. The fundamental objective of MOST suburban communities in attracting new industries is to

    A. increase local employment opportunities
    B. attract minority groups to relocate
    C. establish a balanced land use pattern
    D. increase tax income

29. Which of the following terms is NOT considered to be part of the street classification system?

    A. Major street
    B. Right-of-way
    C. Local street
    D. Cul-de-sac

30. The USUAL purpose for providing a water tower in a municipal water supply system is to

    A. establish a constant pressure
    B. increase the supply of water
    C. increase water pressure
    D. provide a reserve supply

31. The neighborhood unit concept, which includes the elementary school as its major element, was FIRST advocated in 1929 by

    A. Clarence Stein
    B. Henry Wright
    C. Clarence Perry
    D. N. Engelhardt

32. In the past few years, the type of housing which has received the LEAST amount of consideration in resolving the housing problem is

    A. cluster housing
    B. urban renewal
    C. public housing
    D. middle-income housing

33. *Performance standards* have become an INTEGRAL part of zoning ordinances relating to

    A. road construction
    B. industrial districts
    C. parking garages
    D. commercial areas

34. The legal concept upon which the exercise of *condemnation* is based is called the

    A. *due process* clause of the Constitution
    B. police power
    C. power of eminent domain
    D. general community welfare

35. In which of the following situations would the granting of a zoning variance be considered as IMPROPER action? A(n)

    A. serious topographic condition
    B. undersized lot held prior to zoning
    C. subsurface water condition
    D. economic loss due to a zone change

KEY (CORRECT ANSWERS)

1.	D	16.	C
2.	B	17.	D
3.	C	18.	B
4.	D	19.	B
5.	A	20.	C
6.	D	21.	A
7.	C	22.	D
8.	B	23.	B
9.	C	24.	A
10.	B	25.	C
11.	B	26.	C
12.	C	27.	A
13.	A	28.	D
14.	C	29.	B
15.	B	30.	A
31.	C		
32.	C		
33.	B		
34.	C		
35.	D		

TEST 3

DIRECTIONS: Each question or incomplete statement is followed by several suggested answers or completions. Select the one that BEST answers the question or completes the statement. *PRINT THE LETTER OF THE CORRECT ANSWER IN THE SPACE AT THE RIGHT.*

1. The MAJOR objective of cluster zoning is to provide

    A. greater densities
    B. a variety of housing types
    C. open space
    D. racial balance

    1.____

2. One tool in combating the problems of *spread city* is to provide

    A. improved mass transportation systems
    B. more major highways
    C. more single-family detached houses
    D. more community facilities

    2.____

3. The Environmental Protection Agency has issued national air quality standards for six common pollutants. The one of the following pollutants NOT included is

    A. sulfur oxides   B. carbon monoxide
    C. sulfur dioxide   D. hydrocarbon oxides

    3.____

4. The national air quality standards have been issued in two parts: primary and secondary standards. A PRIMARY standard is designed to

    A. protect public health
    B. protect public welfare
    C. establish ambient air quality
    D. prevent damage to the environment

    4.____

5. The MAJOR source of air pollution in many urban areas, according to the Environmental Protection Agency, is

    A. emissions from new plants
    B. fossil-fueled steam-generating plants
    C. motor vehicles
    D. large incinerators

    5.____

6. A technique designed for the analysis of national economies and which employs an industry interaction model appearing in the form of a multi-sector or industrial matrix is called

    A. economic base theory
    B. industrial complex analysis
    C. calculated forecasting
    D. input-output theory

    6.____

7. The traditional master plan, with its strong emphasis on physical improvements, is being more frequently replaced by

   A. policies planning
   B. normative planning
   C. quantitative analysis
   D. flexible planning

8. *Advocate planning* involves the planner in

   A. participating on a federal level to influence local officials
   B. working within the planning unit to obtain his desired goals
   C. working as a citizen, often as a protagonist against the local government
   D. preparing mathematical models of urban development

9. Of the following, the type of commercial development which is LEAST likely to be planned is a

   A. regional shopping center
   B. local shopping complex
   C. highway strip development
   D. central business district

10. The *official map* of a community designates all of the following EXCEPT

    A. street right-of-ways
    B. parks and playgrounds
    C. residential areas
    D. school sites

11. Land use intensity standards are MOST appropriately utilized with the development of

    A. standard subdivisions
    B. planned unit developments
    C. mobile home parks
    D. high-rise residential complexes

12. A topographic map does NOT generally express

    A. climatic conditions
    B. easements
    C. boundary lines and distances
    D. existing buildings

13. Clarence Stein contributed GREATLY to the development of

    A. the concept of the balanced community
    B. the design of Reston
    C. high-rise residential complexes
    D. the Radburn Plan

14. In site development, a 10% grade is considered MAXIMUM for

    A. streets and roads
    B. play fields
    C. building sites
    D. parking lots

15. The Model Cities Program includes all of the following EXCEPT

    A. job training in construction work
    B. local control of programs
    C. physical and social rehabilitation of a community
    D. new city design and development

16. HUD's *Operation Breakthrough* program encouraged

    A. fireproof buildings
    B. innovative prefabricated systems of construction
    C. speed of building erection
    D. a socio-economic assault on the housing program

17. A condominium can BEST be described as a

    A. high-rise residential complex with a complete range of amenities
    B. variation of cooperative ownership
    C. planned unit development with open space
    D. building with full ownership of the dwelling unit and common ownership of public areas

18. A MAJOR advantage of a leaching cesspool is that it

    A. can be used where ground water is two feet below grade
    B. can be used close to potable water
    C. requires a minimum of land area
    D. is limited in capacity

19. Land which rises 2 feet vertically to 5 feet horizontally has a slope of

    A. 2.5%   B. 20%   C. 25%   D. 40%

20. The MAJOR advantage of a subsoil disposal bed for sewage disposal is that it

    A. may be used in any soil except that rated as impervious
    B. is more economical to build
    C. requires less land area than that of a treatment plant
    D. may have a ground water level less than 2 feet below grade

21. To achieve the GREATEST amount of open space in the siting of houses, the one of the following patterns that a planner would MOST probably choose is a _____ pattern.

    A. gridiron   B. court
    C. cluster   D. free-form

22. The maximum distance a child should be required to walk to an elementary school is GENERALLY considered to be _____ mile.

    A. 1/4   B. 1/2   C. 3/4   D. 1

23. Modern industrial parks most often will include all of the following amenities EXCEPT

    A. landscaping and screening
    B. employee parking areas
    C. utilities and services
    D. multi-story structures

24. The BEST source of aerial photographs that provide the greatest coverage of the United States by a single agency is the

    A. Soil Conservation Service
    B. U.S. National Ocean Survey
    C. National Park Service
    D. Agricultural Stabilization Conservation Service

25. Terrain analysis is MOST closely related to the study of

    A. landforms
    B. drainage
    C. soil
    D. land erosion

26. Riparian rights deal with property that is located

    A. over mineral resources
    B. along a body of water
    C. over railroad tracks
    D. over a right-of-way

27. The ADVANTAGE of a *stol* port is that it

    A. can be located near another airport
    B. is not government regulated
    C. accommodates business and pleasure aircraft
    D. requires a short runway

28. One square mile contains EXACTLY _____ acres.

    A. 316   B. 444   C. 640   D. 1,000

29. The one of the following methods of refuse disposal that causes the LEAST air pollution, if efficiently carried out, is

    A. open dumping
    B. land fill
    C. incineration
    D. compositing

30. Sewers which collect sewage only from the plumbing systems of buildings and carry it to a sewage treatment plant are called _____ sewers.

    A. sanitary
    B. storm
    C. combined
    D. constant-flow

KEY (CORRECT ANSWERS)

1. C
2. A
3. C
4. A
5. C

6. D
7. A
8. C
9. C
10. C

11. B
12. A
13. D
14. A
15. D

16. B
17. D
18. C
19. D
20. A

21. C
22. B
23. D
24. D
25. A

26. B
27. D
28. C
29. B
30. A

EXAMINATION SECTION
TEST 1

DIRECTIONS: Each question or incomplete statement is followed by several suggested answers or completions. Select the one that BEST answers the question or completes the statement. *PRINT THE LETTER OF THE CORRECT ANSWER IN THE SPACE AT THE RIGHT.*

1. The Model Cities program, which was authorized by the *Demonstration Cities and Metropolitan Development Act* was designed to

    A. help selected areas plan, administer, and carry out coordinated physical and social programs to improve the environment
    B. aid non-profit organizations to develop and demonstrate new ways of providing housing for low-income families
    C. encourage architects and builders to devise new large-scale construction techniques
    D. offer an alternative to usual urban renewal procedures through funding specific renewal activities on a yearly basis

2. The MAJOR purpose of the capital budgeting process in local government is to

    A. provide operating funds for the various departments
    B. centralize budget decision power in the executive branch
    C. centralize budget decision power in the Council
    D. establish a rational system of priorities for construction

3. The economic base of a community is

    A. the number of wealthy people with annual earnings in excess of $100,000 per year as a ratio to the total population
    B. the percentage of factory employed residents as a ratio of the total work force
    C. the productive industries located within the boundaries of a community
    D. those activities which provide the basic employment and income on which the rest of the local economy depends

4. One of the reasons for the creation of *superagencies* within city government was to

    A. create agencies that would serve as liaisons between the mayor's office and the community
    B. decentralize some of the functions for which the old agencies formerly had responsibility
    C. make each agency autonomous
    D. eliminate duplication of activities among different agencies

5. The word *autonomy* means

    A. automatic
    B. disregard of externals
    C. unlimited power or authority
    D. independent, self-governing

6. De facto, as in de facto segregation, means

   A. by right, in accordance with law
   B. actual
   C. disguised
   D. unintentional

7. American cities gain their legal powers from

   A. the Federal government
   B. the State government
   C. the United States Constitution
   D. common law

8. In an average urban area, the one of the following land uses that would account for the LARGEST percentage of land is

   A. residences
   B. streets
   C. business and industry
   D. public and semi-public uses

9. A cul-de-sac street is a

   A. dead-end street terminating in a circular turn-around
   B. loop street branching off from a collector street
   C. narrow street which has become congested as the result of commercial development
   D. gridiron street on which through traffic is prohibited

10. In the city, the capital budget is initially prepared by the

    A. city council
    B. comptroller
    C. city planning commission
    D. budget director

11. Reasonably well-to-do residential communities have joined the search for non-residential taxpayers but have shown LEAST inclination to plan for

    A. the necessary public utilities
    B. adequate access to the sites
    C. housing the workers
    D. the Budget Director

12. The GREATEST percentage of the daytime population of the business center of the city arrives by

    A. railroad
    B. subway
    C. bus
    D. passenger car

13. The LARGEST single public expenditure in most cities and suburbs in the State is for

    A. schools and education
    B. highways
    C. hospitals and health facilities
    D. police protection

14. The legal basis of zoning is

    A. the police power
    B. the power to levy taxes
    C. the Federal Constitution
    D. a special act of Congress

15. A drug used in addiction programs as a substitute for heroin is

    A. benzedrine
    B. librium
    C. methadone
    D. methanimine

16. The STOLcraft is a(n)

    A. high speed hydrofoil proposed as an alternative to the use of the ferry
    B. vehicle which travels just above the surface of either land or water on a cushion of air
    C. airplane intended for short distance trips between city centers
    D. cargo ship for containerized freight

Questions 17-21.

DIRECTIONS: Questions 17 through 21 are to be answered on the basis of the following information.

FLOOR AREA

Floor area is the sum of the gross areas of the several floors of a building or buildings, measured from the exterior faces of exterior walls or from the center lines of walls separating two buildings.

FLOOR AREA RATIO

Floor area ratio is the total floor area on a zoning lot, divided by the lot area of that zoning lot. (For example, a building containing 20,000 square feet of floor area on a zoning lot of 10,000 square feet has a floor area ratio of 2.0.) Expressed as a formula:

$$FAR = \frac{Floor\ Area}{Lot\ Area}$$

OPEN SPACE RATIO

The *open space ratio* of a zoning lot is the number of square feet of open space on the zoning lot, expressed as a percentage of the floor area on that zoning lot. (For example, if for a particular building an open space ratio of 20 is required, 20,000 square feet of floor area in the building would necessitate 4,000 square feet of open space on the zoning lot upon which the building stands, or, if 6,000 square feet of lot area were in open space, 30,000 square feet of floor area could be in the building on that zoning lot.) Each square foot of open space per 100 square feet of floor area is referred to as one point.

Expressed as a formula:

$$OSR = \frac{100 \times open\ space}{Floor\ Area}$$

17. If a building can be built with a maximum floor area ratio (FAR) of 10.0, this means   17.___

    A. the building can have a maximum of ten stories
    B. the maximum ratio of gross square feet of floor area to area of the first floor is 10:1
    C. that open space on the zoning lot must be provided in an amount equal to ten percent of the total floor area of the building
    D. the maximum ratio of gross square feet of floor area to lot area is 10:1

18. If the open space ratio of a particular building is 18.5 and the actual amount of open space is 13,550 square feet, the floor area of the building must be MOST NEARLY   18.___

    A. 250,675   B. 73,243   C. 28,170   D. 79,027

19. Given: A housing site of 43,560 square feet.   19.___
    At an FAR of 3.33, the allowable total floor area of a proposed building would be MOST NEARLY

    A. 30,736   B. 484,482   C. 48,448   D. 145,055

20. Given: A housing site of 43,560 square feet.   20.___
    At an FAR of 2.94 and an open space ratio of 24.0, how much open space must be provided?

    A. 30,736   B. 10,454   C. 14,816   D. 18,150

21. Given: A housing site of 43,560 square feet.   21.___
    If a proposed building on this site were to have 122,839 gross square feet of floor space, what would the FAR be?

    A. 10.0
    B. 25.5
    C. 2.82
    D. Cannot be determined from data given

Questions 22-24.

DIRECTIONS: Questions 22 through 24 are to be answered on the basis of the following table.

The age characteristics of the total population in a certain neighborhood are as follows:

Age	Number of People
3	2
5	4
12	3
18	3
20	1
21	3
22	4
50	2
56	1
72	2

22. The mean age of the population in the neighborhood described above is MOST NEARLY   22.____

    A. 15   B. 19   C. 23   D. 27

23. The median age of the population in the neighborhood described above is MOST   23.____
    NEARLY

    A. 15   B. 20   C. 25   D. 30

24. The percentage of the population over age 65 in the neighborhood described above is   24.____
    MOST NEARLY

    A. 2   B. 4   C. 6   D. 8

25.   25.____

    [Diagram: a large rectangle containing a smaller rectangle labeled "TOWER"; width marked as 800 ft]

    Assume that the above drawing has been made to scale. The total gross floor area of the 20-story tower is, in square feet, MOST NEARLY

    A. 200,000   B. 100,000   C. 1,000   D. 50,000

KEY (CORRECT ANSWERS)

1.	A	11.	C
2.	D	12.	B
3.	D	13.	A
4.	D	14.	A
5.	D	15.	C
6.	B	16.	C
7.	B	17.	D
8.	A	18.	B
9.	A	19.	D
10.	C	20.	A

21. C
22. C
23. B
24. D
25. A

TEST 2

DIRECTIONS: Each question or incomplete statement is followed by several suggested answers or completions. Select the one that BEST answers the question or completes the statement. *PRINT THE LETTER OF THE CORRECT ANSWER IN THE SPACE AT THE RIGHT.*

1. In the city, the body that is responsible for choosing the specific location of sites for public improvement is the

    A. city planning commission
    B. department of public works
    C. site selection board
    D. fine arts commission

    1.____

2. Publicly-sponsored Early Childhood programs in the city do NOT include

    A. Family Day Care
    B. Headstart Program
    C. playschools for 2- and 3-year olds
    D. pre-kindergarten in elementary schools

    2.____

3. The one of the following that is NOT a current method of controlling pollution is the

    A. requirement that incinerators in the city be upgraded
    B. project for recycling waste paper and aluminum goods for re-use
    C. sale of non-leaded gasoline for automobiles
    D. conversion of all combined sewers in the city to separate sanitary and storm sewers

    3.____

4. In general, the MOST accurate 5-year projection of population can be made for the

    A. nation   B. metropolitan area
    C. inner city   D. neighborhood

    4.____

5. The type of area in which the GREATEST percentage increase in population occurred between 1960 and 1980 was in the

    A. central cities   B. suburban rings
    C. rural non-farm areas D. rural farm areas

    5.____

6. The one of the following that should NOT be included in a community planning study undertaken by a city planning department is

    A. a survey of how land is used in the area
    B. compilation of data on school utilization
    C. determination of rent levels in the area
    D. renovation of an old building at rents suitable for low-income people

    6.____

7. The one of the following men who had a role in laying out cities along the formal lines of the *City Beautiful* movement was

    A. Rexford Tugwell   B. Daniel Burnham
    C. Clarence Stein   D. Frank Lloyd Wright

    7.____

8. A key factor leading to the development of suburban growth in recent decades is

   A. a series of regional government compacts
   B. the large increase in automobile ownership
   C. the drying up of immigration
   D. the gradual shifting of some shopping and employment from the center of the city to the outskirts

9. A controlled aerial mosaic photograph would be LEAST useful in which of the following types of planning work?

   A. Land use study of undeveloped land
   B. Review of subdivision plats
   C. Study of proposed highway locations
   D. Building condition study of CBD

10. The MAJOR function of the city community planning boards is

    A. to prepare capital and expense budgets for community planning districts
    B. to advise the county executives and city agencies on planning issues
    C. as an umbrella organization for local poverty groups
    D. to provide technical planning help to local community groups

11. Special revenue sharing is intended to

    A. be available only for cities of over 1 million population
    B. be available for general purpose use, to be determined by the cities
    C. replace money previously distributed to cities for categorical grants
    D. in all instances be passed from the state to the city

12. The city's water pollution control plants are being upgraded to _____ treatment which removes _____.

    A. primary; "approximately" 65% of pollutants
    B. secondary; approximately 90% of pollutants
    C. tertiary; approximately 99% of pollutants
    D. desalination; all the mineral matter

13. *Turnkey* housing refers to

    A. a method of housing construction whereby a private developer finances and constructs the housing to the city's standards and the housing is then purchased by the city
    B. the conversion of old-law housing to co-op housing in moderate rent areas, including rent subsidies for low-income families
    C. brownstone renovation with no public subsidy in historic districts where the design must be approved by the landmarks commission
    D. a form of mixing housing with commercial or industrial space, as in the incentive zoning amendment

14. The Planned-Unit Development is a provision of the city zoning resolution which   14._____

    A. provides for industrial development on the outskirts of the city
    B. requires the building of schools, community centers, and shopping facilities as part of a large residential development
    C. permits housing to be built close together in clusters, leaving substantial land areas in their natural state as common open spaces
    D. provides a means of constructing off-street parking facilities in high density residential neighborhoods

15. The official map differs from the master plan in that it   15._____

    A. deals only with proposed streets as they relate to existing streets
    B. includes a detailed engineering design for the existing and proposed street system
    C. is an accurate description of the location of public improvements existing and proposed
    D. is tied directly to the Capital Budget and Improvement Program

16. According to the zoning resolution, a legal non-conforming use in zoning is one established   16._____

    A. prior to the adoption of the ordinance provision prohibiting it
    B. by a special exception permit issued by the planning commission
    C. by a variance issued by the board of standards and appeals
    D. for many years despite the prohibition in the ordinance and which had not been proceeded against

17. The formula for financing interstate highways under state and Federal law provides that the government of the city shall pay what percent of the cost of highway construction?   17._____

    A. 100%   B. 90%   C. 40%   D. 0%

18. The one of the following statements that MOST NEARLY expresses the city's long-term program in regard to arterial highways is to   18._____

    A. provide many routes throughout the city in order to minimize travel time from all points
    B. provide quick vehicular access from the business center to the suburbs
    C. build up bypass routes to discourage traffic from entering the business center
    D. build up the highway network in the outer boroughs and to landbank land in the business center for future through routes

19. The city planning commission   19._____

    A. consists of lifetime members, who annually elect a chairman
    B. administers the zoning resolution and hears appeals for variances
    C. prepares the annual 5-year capital improvement plan
    D. prepares the architectural designs for all public buildings, except schools

20. The feature of the city zoning resolution before 1961 which gave the city's skyscrapers their MOST distinctive architectural character was its

    A. height bonus for added setbacks
    B. rear yard provisions
    C. off-street parking and loading requirements
    D. density restrictions

20.____

KEY (CORRECT ANSWERS)

1.	C	11.	C
2.	C	12.	B
3.	D	13.	A
4.	A	14.	C
5.	B	15.	A
6.	D	16.	A
7.	B	17.	D
8.	B	18.	C
9.	D	19.	C
10.	B	20.	A

TEST 3

DIRECTIONS: Each question or incomplete statement is followed by several suggested answers or completions. Select the one that BEST answers the question or completes the statement. *PRINT THE LETTER OF THE CORRECT ANSWER IN THE SPACE AT THE RIGHT.*

Questions 1-3.

DIRECTIONS: Questions 1 through 3, inclusive, are to be answered in accordance with the following paragraphs.

Into the nine square miles that make up Manhattan's business districts, about two million people travel each weekday to go to work — the equivalent of the combined populations of Boston, Baltimore, and Cincinnati. Some 140,000 drive there in cars, 200,000 take buses, and 100,000 ride the commuter railroads. The great majority, however, go by subway — approximately 1.4 million people.

It is some ride. The last major improvement in the subway system was completed in 1935. The subways are dirty and noisy. Many local lines operate well beneath capacity; but many express lines are strained way beyond capacity in particular, the lines to Manhattan, now overloaded by 39,000 passengers during peak hours.

But for all its discomforts, the subway system is inherently a far more efficient way of moving people than automobiles and highways. Making this system faster, more convenient, and more comfortable for people must be the core of the city's transportation effort.

1. The CENTRAL point of the above text is that 1.____
   A. the equivalent of the combined populations of Boston, Baltimore, and Cincinnati commute into Manhattan's business district each weekday
   B. the improvement of the subway system is the key to the solution of moving people efficiently in and out of Manhattan's business district
   C. the subways are dirty and noisy, resulting in a terrible ride
   D. we should increase the ability of people to get in and out of Manhattan by cars, subways, and commuter railroads in order to ease the load from the subways

2. In accordance with the above paragraphs, 1.4 million people commute by subway and 2.____
   _____ by other mass transportation means.
   A. 200,000   B. 100,000   C. 440,000   D. 300,000

3. From the information given in the above paragraphs, one could logically conclude that, next to the subways, the transportation system that carries the LARGEST number of passengers is (the) 3.____
   A. railroads   B. cars
   C. buses   D. local lines

Questions 4-6.

DIRECTIONS: Questions 4 through 6, inclusive, are to be answered in accordance with the following paragraphs.

Incentive zoning is an affirmative tool that has widespread applications. The Zoning Resolution which became effective in 1981 substantially reduced the amount of floor space that a developer could put up on a given size lot and increased the light and air. In the Chrysler Building, which was built under the old legislation, the floor space is 27 times the size of the lot. The maximum ratio allowed for buildings now without a special permit is 18.

The newer zoning ordinance provided incentives to developers to devote part of the plot to public plazas or arcades. This space is needed to supplement the sidewalks, which in many cases are as narrow as they were when the midtown area was lined with brownstone or brickfront houses.

While the newer zoning has produced plazas, it has not of itself proved to be a sufficient development control. Stretches of Third Avenue and the Avenue of the Americas, for example, have been almost completely redeveloped in the last few years. This massive private investment has produced several fine individual buildings. The total environment produced, however, has been disappointing in a number of respects, and there is nowhere near the amenity that there could have been.

4. According to the paragraphs above, the use of incentive zoning has not been entirely successful because it has

    A. discouraged redevelopment
    B. encouraged massive private development along Third Avenue
    C. been ineffective in controlling overall redevelopment
    D. not significantly increased the number of parks and plazas being built

5. According to the above paragraphs, one might conclude that before the new Zoning Resolution was passed,

    A. buildings on a given site were required to have greater setbacks
    B. the amount of private investment in development was significantly smaller than it is today
    C. no controls on development existed
    D. the provision of parks and plazas was less frequent

6. In the context of the above paragraphs, the word *amenity* means

    A. compliance with regulations
    B. correction of undesirable environmental aspects
    C. responsiveness to guidelines and incentives
    D. pleasant or desirable features

Questions 7-8.

DIRECTIONS: Questions 7 and 8 are to be answered in accordance with the following paragraphs.

We must also find better ways to handle the relocation of people uprooted by projects. In the past, many renewal plans have foundered on this problem, and it is still the most difficult part of community development. Large-scale replacement of low-income residents — many ineligible for public housing — has contributed to deterioration of surrounding communities, as in Manhattan's West Side, Coney Island, and Arverne. Recently, thanks to changes in Housing Authority procedures, relocation has been accomplished in a far more satisfactory fashion. The step-by-step community development projects we advocate in this plan should bring further improvement.

But additional measures will be necessary. There are going to be more people to be moved; and, with the current shortage of apartments, large ones especially, it is going to be tougher to find places to move them to. The city should have more freedom to buy or lease housing that comes on the market because of normal turnover and make it available to relocatees.

7. According to the above paragraphs, one of the reasons a neighborhood may deteriorate is that   7._____

    A. there is a scarcity of large apartments
    B. step-by-step community development projects have failed
    C. people in the given neighborhood are uprooted from their homes
    D. a nearby renewal project has an inadequate relocation plan

8. From the above paragraphs, one might conclude that the relocation phase of community renewal has been improved   8._____

    A. by changes in Housing Authority procedures
    B. by development of step-by-step community development projects
    C. through expanded city powers to buy housing for relocation
    D. through the Housing Authority Leasing Program

Questions 9-10.

DIRECTIONS: Questions 9 and 10 are to be answered in accordance with the following paragraphs.

Provision of decent housing for the lower half of the population (by income) was thus taken on as a public responsibility. Public housing was to assist the poorest quarter of urban families while the 221(d)(3) Housing Program would assist the next quarter. But limited funds meant that the supply of subsidized housing could not stretch nearly far enough to help this half of the population. Who were to be left out in the rationing process which was accomplished by the sifting of applicants for housing on the part of public and private authorities?

Discrimination on the grounds of race or color is not allowed under Federal law. In all sections of the country, encouragingly, housing programs are found which allow this law to the letter. Yet, housing programs in some cities still suffer from the residue of racial segregation policies and attitudes that for years were condoned or even encouraged.

Some sifting in the 221(d)(3) Housing Program follows the practice of many public housing authorities, the imposition of requirements with respect to character. This is a delicate matter. To fill a project overwhelmingly with broken families, alcoholics, criminals, delinquents, and other problem tenants would hardly make it a wholesome environment. Yet the total exclusion of such families is hardly an acceptable alternative. To the extent this exclusion is practiced, the very people whose lives are described in order to persuade lawmakers and the public to instigate new programs find the door shut in their faces when such programs come into being. The proper balance is difficult to achieve, but society's neediest families surely should not be totally denied the opportunities for rejuvenation in subsidized housing.

9. From the above paragraphs, it can be assumed that the 221(d)(3) Housing Program

   A. served a population earning more than the median income
   B. served a less affluent population than is served by public housing
   C. excludes all problem families from its projects
   D. is a subsidized housing program

10. According to the above paragraphs, the provision of housing for the poor

    A. has not been completely accomplished with public monies
    B. is never influenced by segregationist policies
    C. is limited to providing housing for only the neediest families
    D. is primarily the responsibility of the Federal government

Questions 11-12.

DIRECTIONS: Questions 11 and 12 are to be answered in accordance with the following paragraph.

Though the recent trend toward apartment construction may appear to be the region's response to large-lot zoning and centralized industry, it really is not. It is mainly a function of the age of the population (coupled with a rush to build apartments in the city between the passage of the newer zoning ordinance and its enforcement in December 1981). Most of the apartments are occupied by one- and two-person families — young people out of school but without a family of their own and older people whose children have grown. Both groups have been increasing in number; and, in this region, they characteristically live in apartments. It is this increased demand for apartments and the simultaneous decrease in demand for one-family houses that dramatically raised the percentage of building permits issued for multi-family housing units from 36 percent in 1977 to 67 percent in 1981. The fact that three-fourths of the apartments were built in the Core between 1977 and 1981 at the same time as the Core was losing population underscores the failure of the apartment boom to slow the outward spread of the population.

11. According to the above paragraph, one of the reasons for the increase in the number of building permits issued for multi-family construction in the city metropolitan region is

    A. that workers in industry want to live close to their jobs
    B. an increase in the number of elderly people living in the region
    C. the inability of many families to afford the large lots necessary to build private homes
    D. the new zoning ordinance made it easier to build apartments

12. According to the above paragraph, the apartment construction boom

    A. increased the population density in the core
    B. spurred a population shift to the suburbs
    C. did not halt the outward flow of the population from the core
    D. was most significant in the outer areas of the region

Questions 13-14.

DIRECTIONS: Questions 13 and 14 are to be answered in accordance with the following paragraphs.

The city's economy has its own dynamics, and there is only so much the government can do to shape it. But that margin is critically important. If the city uses its points of leverage, it can generate a large number of jobs and good jobs, jobs that lead to advancement.

As a major employer itself, the city can upgrade the jobs it offers and greatly improve its services to the public if it does so. Since highly skilled professionals will always be in short supply, the city must train more paraprofessionals to take over routine tasks. Equally important, it must provide them with a realistic job ladder so they can move on up — nurse's aide to certified nurse, for example, teacher's aide to teacher. The training programs for such upgrading will require a substantial public investment but the cost-benefit return should be excellent.

As a major purchaser of goods and services, the city can stimulate business enterprise in the ghetto. The growth of Black and Puerto Rican firms will produce more local jobs; it will also create the kind of managerial talent the ghetto needs.

New kinds of enterprise can be set up. In housing, for example, there is a huge backlog of rehabilitation work to be done and a large pool of unskilled manpower to be trained for it. Corporations can be formed to take over tenements, remodel, maintain, and operate them, as in the Brownsville Home Maintenance Program. Grocery cooperatives to bring food prices down are another possibility.

13. According to the above paragraphs, the city is the major employer and, by using its capacity, it can

    A. assist unskilled people with talent to move up on the job ladder
    B. create private enterprises that will renew all areas of the city in need of renewal
    C. eliminate poverty in the ghetto areas by selective purchase of goods and services
    D. have no influence on the economy of the city

14. According to the above paragraphs, one may REASONABLY conclude that

    A. the city has no power to influence the job market
    B. a by-product of strategic purchasing and employment and training practices can be the rehabilitation of housing and the lowering of food prices
    C. highly skilled professions, which are now in short supply, will no longer be needed after paraprofessionals are trained to take over routine jobs
    D. the city's major objective is to bring down food prices

15. 500 persons attended a public hearing at which a proposed public housing project was being considered. Less than half favored the project, while the majority opposed the project.
    According to the above statement, it is REASONABLE to conclude that

    A. the proposal stimulated considerable community interest
    B. the public housing project was disapproved by the city because a majority opposed it

C. those who opposed the project lacked sympathy for needy persons
D. the supporters of the project were led by militants

16. A document was published by a public agency and distributed for discussion. The document contained data showing trends in the level of reading among freshmen college students and suggested that the high schools were not investing enough effort in overcoming retardation. It compared the costs of intensifying reading instruction in the secondary schools as compared to costs in college for such instruction.
According to the above statement, it is REASONABLE to conclude that

   A. the document proposed new programs
   B. the college students read better than high school students
   C. some college students need remedial reading
   D. the study was done by a consultant

17. A vacant lot close to a polluted creek is for sale. Two buyers compete. One owns an adjacent factory which provides 300 high paying unskilled jobs. He needs to expand or move from the city. If he expands, he will provide 300 additional jobs. The other is a community group in a changing residential area close by. They hope to stabilize the neighborhood by bringing in new housing. They could build an apartment building with 100 dwelling units on the lot.
According to the above paragraph, it is REASONABLE to conclude that

   A. jobs are more important than housing
   B. there is conflict between the factory owners and the neighborhood group
   C. the neighborhood group will not succeed in stabilizing the area by constructing new housing
   D. the polluted creek should be cleaned up

Questions 18-21.

DIRECTIONS: Questions 18 through 21, inclusive, refer to the phrases shown below. For each of the questions, select that phrase which BEST completes the sentence for that question.

   A. to increase training and educational opportunities
   B. to remove social ills by a slum clearance program
   C. to select the goals and values to which these resources should be directed
   D. to diminish drastic redevelopment, to provide opportunities to move within the area, or to move to new areas which can be assimilated to old objectives

18. In addition to concern with the rational allocation of resources, the urban planning process needs _____.

19. The early housing reformers emphasized the inadequate physical environment of the slums, understressed the connection between the social environment of the slums and the disorders they wanted to cure, and attempted _____.

20. The objective for assisting the transition to middle class status will mean intensified efforts _____. 20.____

21. To provide a sense of continuity for those people whose residential areas are being renewed, mainly working class, it is desirable _____. 21.____

Questions 22-25.

DIRECTIONS: For Questions 22 through 25, select that item from Column B that is MOST closely related to the item in Column A.

COLUMN A   COLUMN B

22. City Map   A. Citizen Participation   22.____
23. Revenue Sharing   B. Block Grants   23.____
24. Opportunity Structure   C. Streets   24.____
25. Public Hearing   D. Upward Mobility   25.____

KEY (CORRECT ANSWERS)

1.	B	11.	B
2.	D	12.	C
3.	C	13.	A
4.	C	14.	B
5.	D	15.	A
6.	D	16.	C
7.	D	17.	B
8.	A	18.	C
9.	D	19.	B
10.	A	20.	A

21. D
22. C
23. B
24. D
25. A

EXAMINATION SECTION
TEST 1

DIRECTIONS: Each question or incomplete statement is followed by several suggested answers or completions. Select the one that BEST answers the question or completes the statement. *PRINT THE LETTER OF THE CORRECT ANSWER IN THE SPACE AT THE RIGHT.*

1. Ebenezer Howard is BEST known for the concept of self-sufficient towns with mixed economies which are called

   A. new towns
   B. garden cities
   C. planned unit developments
   D. suburbs

2. The new town of Columbia, Maryland, has which of the following planned features?
   I. Neighborhood clusters
   II. A rail commuter system
   III. Prior land assembly
   IV. Prohibition of industry

   The CORRECT answer is:

   A. II only   B. I, III   C. II, IV   D. I, III, IV

3. The two lines on the graph shown at the right BEST represent which of the following combinations of travel behavior in a metropolitan area of 2 million population?

   A. Transit and private automobile trips
   B. Weekday and weekend trips
   C. All work and nonwork trips
   D. Office and retail-generated trips

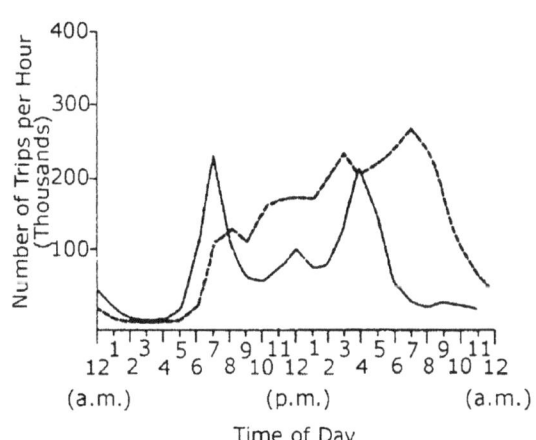

4. Assume that you are the director of a local planning agency, and that you recognize the interdependency of the chief executive, the planning agency, operating departments, and independent boards and commissions. In a hypothetical situation, a proposed expansion of a county airport and adjacent industrial areas is in opposition to the planning agency's proposal for a regional park location.
The planning agency believes there are unique circumstances and sound reasons for preferring the regional park proposal along with future relocation of the airport to another site in the county.
Which of the following strategies would likely place you, as the planning director, in the LEAST effective coordinating role in resolving the conflict?

A. Attempting to have the planning agency solely responsible for additional studies and recommendations
B. Directing planning staff to discontinue all studies of this issue and direct all inquiries regarding this matter to the director
C. Recommending the study control be given to the staff of the chief executive's office
D. Soliciting support of other departments and agencies for the planning agency's regional park proposal

5. Recent major developments in household characteristics in the United States have been characterized by which of the following?
   I. A marked increase in nonfamily living arrangements among the adult population has been observed in recent years.
   II. A major development in marriage trends has been the sharply decreasing level of divorce in central cities.
   III. Families (households where all members are related) maintained by either men or women who have no spouse living with them represent a growing proportion of all family households.
   IV. After several decades of decline in household size, the number of persons per unit has increased in metropolitan area since 1970.

   The CORRECT answer is:

   A. I only B. I, III C. III, IV D. I, II, IV

Questions 6-9.

DIRECTIONS: The group of questions below consists of four lettered headings followed by a list of numbered phrases. For each numbered phrase, select the one heading which is MOST closely related to it. One heading may be used once, more than once, or not at all.

In the following list, which of the formal bodies that operate within a city most likely would take final action on each of the following requests?

   A. City Council
   B. City Court
   C. Board of Zoning Appeals
   D. School Board

6. A request to acquire land for a new school.

7. A request to condemn property in a blighted area.

8. A request to levy a special property assessment for a street.

9. A request for a variance from a zoning ordinance.

10. In reference to the following hypothetical linear regression equation that describes household trip generation with the census tract as the unit of analysis, which of the following statements about R^2 is CORRECT?

   $T = -.65 + .96(p) + .61(v)$
   $R^2 = .69$
   T = the average number of daily vehicle trips from home per DU (dwelling unit)
   p = persons per DU
   v = vehicles per DU

   A. It shows that more p causes households to make more trips.
   B. It shows that more p, only when coupled with more automobiles, causes households to make more trips.
   C. It indicates that 69% of the variation in trip generation is explained by p and v.
   D. There is a 45% probability that the variables T, p, and v are correlated by chance.

10.____

Questions 11-14.

DIRECTIONS: Questions 11 through 14 are to be answered on the basis of the following circumstance.

The desirability and feasibility of a proposed shopping center are to be evaluated. The primary concerns are that conditions of the city zoning ordinance be met and that the project be a profitable venture. The developer owns a 30-acre parcel and proposes to construct a 250,000-square foot leasable area with 1,300 on-site parking spaces. The shopping center will serve a trade area that contains 20,000 households. The average household disposable income is $12,000. The shopping center will have a 50:50 split of square footage between convenience and shopper's goods.

11. Which of the following would be APPROPRIATE in a shopping center of this size?

   A. A major grocery and a drugstore as prime tenants
   B. Either a department or discount store as the anchor tenant
   C. Three department stores of approximately the same size
   D. A series of smaller stores rather than an anchor tenant

11.____

12. If an average of 400 square feet is needed to accommodate each parking space and associated driveways, the APPROXIMATE acreage of the blacktop area of the site would be _____ acres.

   A. Less than 10
   B. Between 10 and 15
   C. Between 15 and 20
   D. More than 20

12.____

13. If 50 percent of disposable income is allocated to retail purchases, a minimum of $100 of sales per square foot is needed to operate profitably, and 750,000 square feet of retail business already exists in the trade area, which of the following should be concluded? The

   A. trade area is already overbuilt and cannot support additional development without further population growth
   B. new shopping center will use up all of the untapped purchasing power of the trade area

13.____

C. existing and proposed centers can operate profitably with excess purchasing power available for additional development
D. trade area is not overbuilt presently, but it can only accommodate an additional 150,000 square feet

14. Provisions in the zoning ordinance require a 4:1 ratioof open space to building space and a 5:1,000-square foot ratio of parking space to gross leasable area (GLA). According to the ordinance, which of the following statements about the parcel is CORRECT?
It is

   A. too small to accommodate the projected center, although adequate parking would be provided
   B. large enough to accommodate the projected center, but parking spaces would be inadequate
   C. large enough to accommodate the projected center, and sufficient parking would be provided
   D. grossly underutilized and could accommodate additional square footage and additional parking spaces

14.____

Questions 15-17.

DIRECTIONS: Questions 15 through 17 are to be answered on the basis of the following information.

Planners in a large city that consists of 150 neighborhoods are concerned about the provision and allocation of health-care clinics at the multiple-neighborhood level throughout the city. One of the main concerns is prenatal health care. Variables relevant to this situation are as follows:
   QPNHC = the overall quality of prenatal health care
   IMR = the percentage of children who survive their first three months of life (a type of infant mortality rate) and who were born in the same one-year period
   NWP = the number of women pregnant at any time during a one-year period
   NA = the number of appointments kept at the health clinic per year
   FI = the family incomes of residents in thousands of dollars ($1,000's)
   D = the distance of families from the health clinics in miles
(Neighborhood averages can be generated for each of these variables.)

15. The planners have decided that the neighborhood infant mortality rate will serve as the operational objective of the prenatal health care system.
Which of the following would be the MOST serious criticism leveled against their decision?

   A. It is impossible to calculate the IMR at the neighborhood level.
   B. The data on the use of the clinic (NA) are easier to obtain and more accurate than the other data.
   C. The IMR is a good quantitative but weak qualitative index of the QPNHC.
   D. The collection of IMR data is irrelevant to the problem.

15.____

16. Which of the following is an output variable within the model?

   A. IMR   B. NWP   C. FI   D. D

16.____

17. It is now 10 years later; the clinics were built and a very comprehensive data collection system was kept in operation. The clinic programs are under fire, the budgets are expected to be slashed, and some clinics probably will be forced to close. Time is short. Based on this situation, which of the following would be the LEAST critical evaluation question?

    A. Are higher levels of clinic usage associated with various infant mortality rates?
    B. If distance does not affect the use of the clinics, does it do so differentially by income strata?
    C. What kinds of persons (education, income level, etc.) use each clinic?
    D. Are family income levels associated with distance

17._____

KEY (CORRECT ANSWERS)

1. B
2. B
3. C
4. B
5. B
6. D
7. A
8. A
9. C
10. C
11. B
12. B
13. C
14. C
15. C
16. A
17. D

GRAPHS, MAPS, SKETCHES

EXAMINATION SECTION
TEST 1

DIRECTIONS: Each question or incomplete statement is followed by several suggested answers or completions. Select the one that BEST answers the question or completes the statement. *PRINT THE LETTER OF THE CORRECT ANSWER IN THE SPACE AT THE RIGHT.*

Questions 1-7.

DIRECTIONS: Questions 1 to 7, inclusive, are based on information contained on Chart A.

1. Puerto Ricans were the LARGEST number of people in

   A. 1975   B. 1973   C. 1979   D. 1971

2. At some time between 1974 and 1975, two groups had the same number of persons. These two groups were

   A. Puerto Rican and Black
   B. Caucasian and Black
   C. Oriental and Black
   D. Puerto Rican and Caucasian

3. In the same year that the Black population reached its GREATEST peak, the LOWEST number of people residing in Revere were of the following group or groups:

   A. Puerto Rican and Caucasian
   B. Oriental
   C. Puerto Rican
   D. Puerto Rican and Oriental

4. The group which showed the GREATEST increase in population from 1970 to 1979 is

   A. Puerto Rican
   B. Caucasian
   C. Oriental
   D. not determinable from the graph

5. In 1977, the Black population was higher by APPROXIMATELY 20% over

   A. 1972   B. 1976   C. 1974   D. 1978

6. The SMALLEST number of people in 1973 were

   A. Puerto Rican and Black
   B. Oriental and Black
   C. Puerto Rican and Caucasian
   D. Puerto Rican and Oriental

7. The percent increase in population of Puerto Ricans from 1971 to 1978 is *most nearly* 7._____
   A. 34% B. 18% C. 62% D. 80%

CHART A

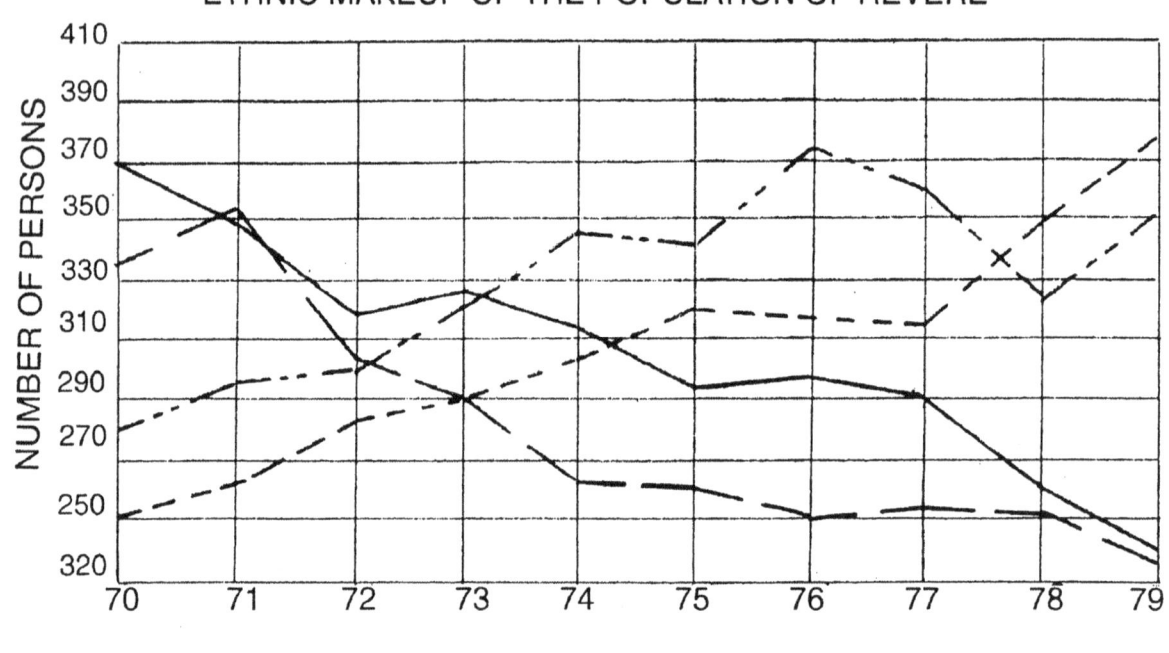

KEY (CORRECT ANSWERS)

1. C
2. D
3. B
4. A
5. A
6. D
7. A

TEST 2

DIRECTIONS: Each question or incomplete statement is followed by several suggested answers or completions. Select the one that BEST answers the question or completes the statement. *PRINT THE LETTER OF THE CORRECT ANSWER IN THE SPACE AT THE RIGHT.*

Questions 1-2.

DIRECTIONS: Questions 1 and 2 are based on information contained on Chart B.

1. The percent of Black middle students attending overcrowded schools in the period 1967 to 1968 is *most nearly*

    A. 34.6 B. 37.6 C. 44.0 D. 47.5

    1.____

2. The percent growth in total school enrollment between 1960-61 and 1967-68 is *most nearly*

    A. 37.6
    B. 45.7
    C. 35.8
    D. cannot be determined from data given

    2.____

CHART B

Summary: School Utilization and Enrollment

PRIMARY SCHOOLS	1960-61	1967-68
NUMBER OF/PERCENT SCHOOLS/UTILIZATION	20/105	20/102
ENROLLMENT/CAPACITY	16685/15842	18204/17813
UTILIZATION: OVER/UNDER	+1942/-1099	+2045/-1654
	NET +843	NET +391
	NO. %	NO. %
WHITE ENROLLMENT	3645 21.8	3146 17.2
NEGRO ENROLLMENT	12691 76.1	14304 78.1
PUERTO RICAN ENROLLMENT	349 2.1	754 4.1

MIDDLE SCHOOLS	1960-61	1967-68
NUMBER OF/PERCENT SCHOOLS/UTILIZATION	3/101	5/96
ENROLLMENT/CAPACITY	4869/4808	7502/7811
UTILIZATION: OVER/UNDER	+235/-174	+276/-585
	NET +61	NET -309
	NO. %	NO. %
WHITE ENROLLMENT	1478 30.4	1717 22.8
NEGRO ENROLLMENT	3279 67.3	5228 69.6
PUERTO RICAN ENROLLMENT	112 2.3	557 7.4

HIGH SCHOOLS	1960-61	1967-68
NUMBER OF/PERCENT SCHOOLS/UTILIZATION	2/78	3/107
ENROLLMENT/CAPACITY	1791/2300	6003/5847
UTILIZATION: OVER/UNDER	+15/-524	+985/-829
	NET -509	NET +156
	NO. %	NO. %
WHITE ENROLLMENT	1106 61.8	3266 54.4
NEGRO ENROLLMENT	650 36.3	2561 42.6
PUERTO RICAN ENROLLMENT	35 2.0	176 2.9

Detail: School Utilization and Enrollment 1967-1968

PRIMARY SCHOOLS	CONSTRUCTION—DATES AND TYPE*	GRADES	AVERAGE YRS OVER OR UNDER GRADE	SPECIAL PROGRMS	ENROLLMENT TOTAL	WHITE NO	WHITE %	NEGRO NO	NEGRO %	PUERTO RICAN NO	PUERTO RICAN %	CAPACITY TOTAL	AVAIL- SHORT+	% UTIL	# OF OTHER UTIL ROOMS
PS 15	1939	K-5	-.1	T,AS	565	2	.3	523	92.5	40	7.0	669	- 104	84.4	
PS 30	1965	K-5	+1.2	T,AS	1605	854	53.2	748	46.6	3	.1	1099	+ 506	146.0	18 (NOTE M)
PS 35	1931	K-5	+.6	AS	640	345	53.9	259	40.4	36	5.6	702	- 62	91.1	6 PORTABLES
PS 36	1924,63	K-5	-.3	SS	703	9	1.2	684	97.2	10	1.4	509	+ 194	138.1	6 PORTABLES
PS 37	1928	K-5	+.1	MES,AS	615	61	9.9	544	88.4	10	1.6	419	+ 196	146.7	
PS 40	1912,42,64	K-5	-.8	SS,MES	1058	9	.8	994	93.9	55	5.1	869	+ 189	121.7	6 (NOTE N)
PS 45	1914,28,63	K-5	-.8	SS	986	7	.7	949	96.2	30	3.0	856	+ 130	115.1	4 PORTABLES
PS 48	1936	K-5	+1.2	SP	495	10	2.0	482	97.3	3	.6	632	- 137	78.3	1 (NOTE O)
PS 50	1922	K-5	-.2	SS	772	116	15.0	593	76.8	63	8.1	833	- 61	92.6	
PS 80	1964	K-5	+1.5	T,AS	1052	421	40.0	574	54.5	57	5.4	1197	- 145	87.8	
PS 82	1906	K-5	-.1		440	375	85.2	21	4.7	44	10.0	378	+ 62	116.4	2 (NOTE P)
PS 95	1915,25	K-5	-.3	SS	1274	489	38.3	647	50.7	138	10.8	1320	- 46	96.5	
PS 116	1925,64	K-5	-.1	SS	914	2	.2	902	98.6	10	1.0	1067	- 153	85.6	
PS 118	1923,32	K-5	+.0	T	887	28	3.1	832	93.7	27	3.0	1089	- 202	81.4	
PS 123	1928,32,64	K-5	-1.2	SS	1565	41	2.6	1448	92.5	76	4.8	1103	+ 462	141.8	17 PORTABLES
PS 134	1928,38	K-5	-.3	T	1067	42	3.9	959	89.8	66	6.1	761	+ 306	140.2	
PS 136	1928,37	K-6	-.6	T	987	10	1.0	950	96.2	27	2.7	1301	- 314	75.8	1 (NOTE Q)
PS 140	1929,38,63	K-5	-.8	SS	1160	46	3.9	1098	94.6	16	1.3	1241	- 81	93.4	
PS 160	1939	K-5	-.1	SS	1019	11	1.0	1006	98.7	2	.1	1030	- 11	98.9	
PS 178	1951	K-6	+1.8		400	268	67.0	91	22.7	41	10.2	738	- 338	54.2	
TOTAL PRIMARY SCHOOLS= 20					18204	3146	17.2	14304	78.5	754	4.1	17813	+2045 / -1654	102.1	

MIDDLE SCHOOLS															
IS 8	1963	6-8	-.5	SS,PI	1562	325	20.8	1124	71.9	113	7.2	1523	+ 39	102.5	
IS 59	1956	6-7	-.1	P,T,AS	1633	621	38.0	846	51.8	166	10.1	1396	+ 237	116.9	
IS 72	1967	6-8	+.1	SS	1396	210	15.0	1171	83.8	15	1.1	1647	- 251	84.7	
IS 142	1930,38	6-8	-1.5		1096	32	1.9	1004	91.6	21	6.4	1333	- 237	82.2	
JS 192	1963	7-9	-.8	SS	1815	540	29.7	1083	59.6	192	10.5	1912	+ 97	94.9	
TOTAL MIDDLE SCHOOLS= 5					7502	1717	22.8	5228	69.6	557	7.4	7811	+ 276 / - 585	96.0	

HIGH SCHOOLS															
SPRINGFLD GDNS	1965	9-12	-.3		4277	2758	64.4	1462	34.1	57	1.3	3292	+ 985	129.9	
JAMAICA VOC¹	1896-C	9-12	-2.9		644	382	59.3	235	36.4	27	4.1	895	- 251	71.9	
M WILSON VOC	1942	9-12	-3.7		1082	126	11.6	864	79.8	92	8.5	1660	- 578	65.1	
TOTAL HIGH SCHOOLS= 3					6003	3266	54.4	2561	42.6	176	2.9	5847	+ 985 / - 829	102.6	

CODE
- T: TRANSITIONAL SCHOOL
- AS: AFTER SCHOOL STUDY CENTER
- SS: SPECIAL SERVICE SCHOOL
- MES: MORE EFFECTIVE SCHOOL
- SP: SPECIAL PRIMARY SCHOOL
- PI: PILOT INTERMEDIATE SCHOOL

NOTES
1. INCLUDES ENROLLMENT AND CAPACITY AT ANNEX (PS 170) IN QUEENS PLANNING DISTRICT 8
* EXCEPT AS NOTED ALL SCHOOLS ARE OF FIREPROOF CONSTRUCTION
C: NOT FIREPROOF
X: NOT AVAILABLE

NOTES
- M: IN ROCHDALE VILLAGE
- N: 4 PORTABLES, 2 IN UNION METHODIST CHURCH
- O: IN BROOKS MEMORIAL METHODIST CHURCH
- P: AT 139-35 88TH STREET
- Q: IN GRACE METHODIST EPISCOPAL CHURCH

KEY (CORRECT ANSWERS)

1. B
2. C

TEST 3

DIRECTIONS: Each question or incomplete statement is followed by several suggested answers or completions. Select the one that BEST answers the question or completes the statement. *PRINT THE LETTER OF THE CORRECT ANSWER IN THE SPACE AT THE RIGHT.*

Questions 1-4.

DIRECTIONS: Questions 1 to 4, inclusive, are based on the information contained on Chart C.

1. What percent of all households in 1960 are Puerto Rican households with incomes of $6,000 or more per year?

    A. 38%   B. 57%   C. 6%   D. 0.6%

    1.____

2. The median income in all households in 1960 is in the range of

    A. $3,000 - $5,999
    B. $6,000 - $9,999
    C. $10,000 - $14,999
    D. cannot be determined from data given

    2.____

3. The total number of white persons living in one or two person households in 1960 is

    A. 13,126   B. 28,884   C. 24,704   D. 46.5

    3.____

4. Which of the following statements is MOST likely to be true?

    A. In 1970, the majority of the population in the above data is white.
    B. The majority of households in 1960 have incomes under $6,000.
    C. There are 8668 people in 1960 in households with incomes under $3,000.
    D. The majority of households in 1960 with incomes under $2,000 are white.

    4.____

CHART C

Population and Housing Data

Housing Units

	TOTAL	1 ROOM	2 ROOMS	3 ROOMS	4 ROOMS	5 ROOMS	6+ ROOMS
TOTAL HOUSING UNITS - 1960	57611	1484	2492	10491	9074	8409	25661
TOTAL OCCUPIED HOUSING UNITS	56187						
RENTER OCCUPIED - TOTAL	23040						
PUBLIC PUBLICLY AIDED	1048	--	44	240	553	199	12
		--	--	--	--	--	--
OWNER OCCUPIED - TOTAL	33147						
PUBLICLY AIDED	--	--	--	--	--	--	--
PUBLIC HOUSING - 1970							
PUBLIC RENTER	1434	--	44	321	736	300	33
PUBLICLY AIDED RENTER	65	--	1	22	26	17	--
PUBLICLY AIDED OWNER	6075	--	3	2770	2214	568	520

Population Growth

(Line graph showing population from 1950 to 1970, Y-axis 0 to 250,000)

Ethnic Make-up (in percent)

(Bar chart showing White ○, Black ●, Puerto Rican * for years 1950, 1960, 1970)

Households 1960 (in percent)

	% OF ALL HOUSEHOLDS	PERSONS IN HOUSEHOLDS					
		1	2	3	4	5	6+
White	56	14	33	21	17	9	7
Black	43	7	23	20	19	13	18
Puerto Rican	1	4	13	17	18	21	27
All Households	100%	12	23	20	17	12	12

Income 1960

	PERSONS IN HOUSEHOLD						TOTAL NUMBER OF HOUSEHOLDS
	1	2	3	4	5+		
WHITE HOUSEHOLDS							
UNDER $2000	1652	1153	276	143	122		3346
$2000 - $2999	459	717	176	67	58		1477
$3000 - $5999	1472	3018	1688	1290	944		8412
$6000 - $9999	501	3520	2649	1936	1906		10506
$10000 - $14999	75	1378	1255	1069	1144		4925
$15000 AND OVER	17	476	535	637	680		2345
NEGRO AND OTHER NON-WHITE HOUSEHOLDS							
UNDER $2000	454	664	366	303	444		2291
$2000 - $2999	237	453	315	192	280		1477
$3000 - $5999	587	2368	1721	1304	2313		8293
$6000 - $9999	98	1735	1984	1650	2465		7932
$10000 - $14999	13	370	547	679	1370		3026
$15000 AND OVER	1	23	82	116	435		656
PUERTO RICAN HOUSEHOLDS							
UNDER $2000	9	7	7	11	11		45
$2000 - $2999	4	1	2	14	12		32
$3000 - $5999	10	17	45	26	71		169
$6000 - $9999	--	42	35	30	112		219
$10000 - $14999	--	8	5	21	53		87
$15000 AND OVER	--	--	4	3	19		26
ALL HOUSEHOLDS							
UNDER $2000	2155	1824	649	457	577		5662
$2000 - $2999	700	1170	493	273	358		2994
$3000 - $5999	2069	5403	3454	2620	1328		16874
$6000 - $9999	599	5297	4668	3616	4477		18657
$10000 - $14999	92	1756	1857	1769	2567		8041
$15000 AND OVER	17	499	621	756	1134		3027

KEY (CORRECT ANSWERS)

1. D
2. B
3. C
4. D

TEST 4

DIRECTIONS: Each question or incomplete statement is followed by several suggested answers or completions. Select the one that BEST answers the question or completes the statement. *PRINT THE LETTER OF THE CORRECT ANSWER IN THE SPACE AT THE RIGHT.*

Questions 1-4.

DIRECTIONS: Questions 1 through 4, inclusive, are based on information contained on Chart D.

1. The percentage of households by ethnic make-up in 1960 was *most nearly*

   A. 16% white, 12% Black and other non-white, 16% Puerto Rican, and 56% not reported
   B. 39% white, 26% Black and other non-white, and 35% Puerto Rican
   C. 95% white, 3% Black and 2% Puerto Rican
   D. 99% white, 1% Black and other non-white, and 0% Puerto Rican

   1.____

2. In 1960, the predominant age group was in the age range of

   A. 5-15   B. 25-44   C. 45-64   D. 0-15

   2.____

3. In 1960, the LARGEST singular and discrete income group consisted of households with the following characteristics:

   A. Black and other non-white households of 3 persons with total earnings of between $6,000 and $9,999
   B. White households with 3 persons with total earnings from under $2,000 to $5,999
   C. White households of 2 persons with total earnings between $6,000 and $9,999
   D. White households with total earnings under $2,000

   3.____

4. The percent population increase between 1950 and 1970 was most nearly

   A. 56%   B. 30%   C. 25%   D. 33%

   4.____

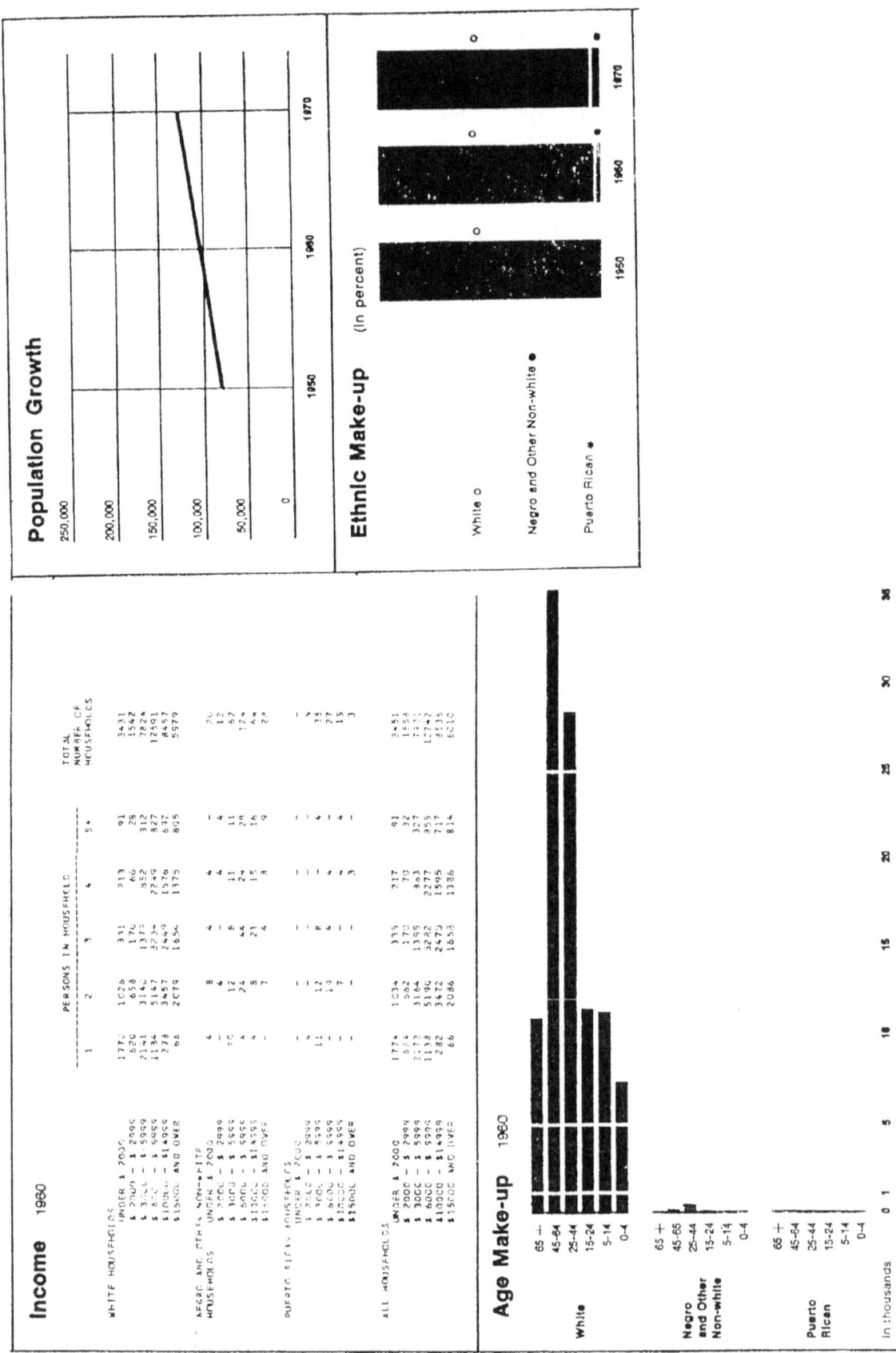

CHART D

KEY (CORRECT ANSWERS)

1. D
2. C
3. C
4. A

TEST 5

DIRECTIONS: Each question or incomplete statement is followed by several suggested answers or completions. Select the one that BEST answers the question or completes the statement. *PRINT THE LETTER OF THE CORRECT ANSWER IN THE SPACE AT THE RIGHT.*

Questions 1-3.

DIRECTIONS: Questions 1 through 3, inclusive, are based on information contained on Zoning Map E. Zoning Map E is drawn to scale. Candidates are to scale off measurements.

1. One-third of Block A (shaded area) has already been developed as a public housing project. It is proposed that a second development be built on the remainder of the site. The approximate size of the proposed site, in acres, is *most nearly* (43,650 sq.ft. = 1 acre)

   A. 5.9 B. 55 C. 1.8 D. 10.3

   1.____

2. If Site B were developed for housing and 40% of the site was covered by buildings, the amount of open space would be *most nearly* _____ acres.

   A. 2.5 B. 6.3 C. 3.8 D. 2.7

   2.____

3. A new elementary school will have to be built to accommodate the children from the two proposed projects at A and B.
If the new school must be within 1/2 mile walk of any point in either project, which would be the *most likely* site?

   A. 1 B. 2 C. 3 D. 4

   3.____

ZONING MAP E

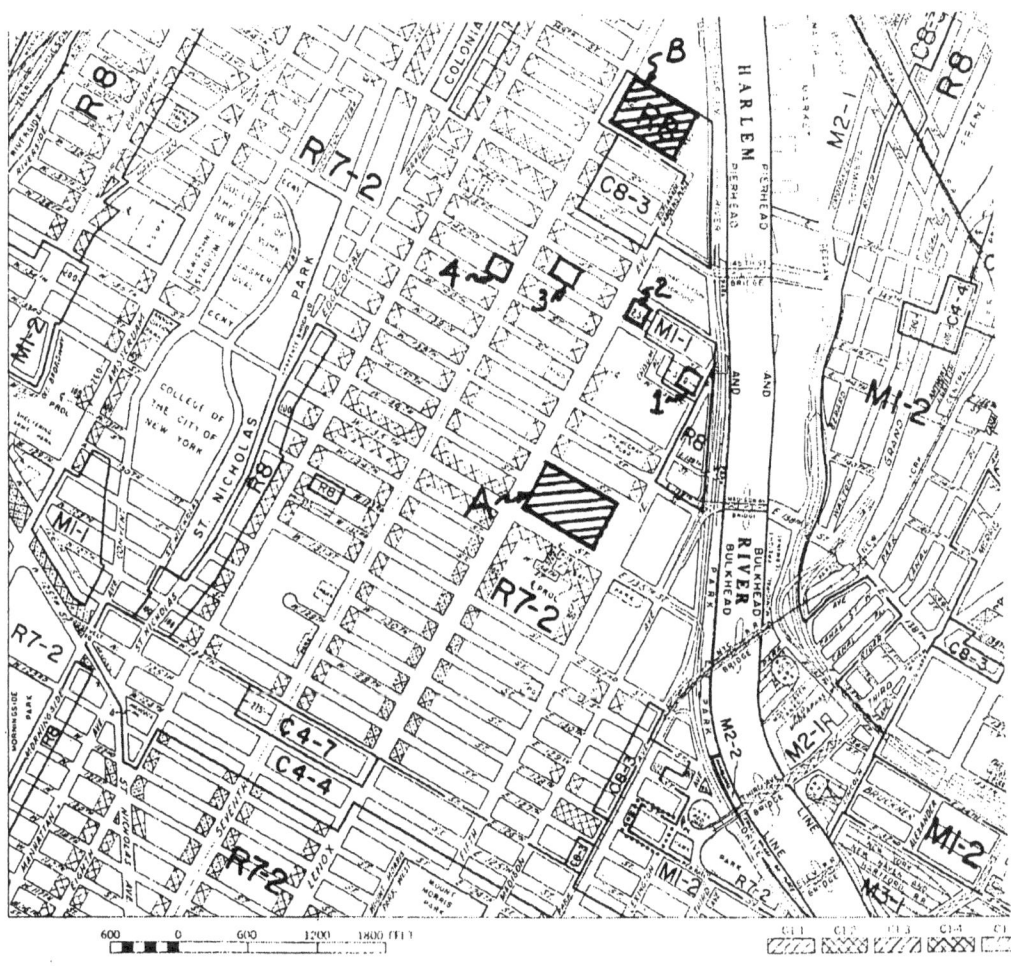

KEY (CORRECT ANSWERS)

1. A
2. C
3. B

TEST 6

DIRECTIONS: Each question or incomplete statement is followed by several suggested answers or completions. Select the one that BEST answers the question or completes the statement. *PRINT THE LETTER OF THE CORRECT ANSWER IN THE SPACE AT THE RIGHT.*

Questions 1-2.

DIRECTIONS: Questions 1 and 2 are to be answered in accordance with the Coast and Geodetic Map F.

1. The difference in elevation between the lowest and highest point of Ewen Park is *most nearly* _____ feet.

   A. 100 B. 25 C. 200 D. 50

2. Given: The scale of the map is as shown.
   The distance between the College of Mt. St. Vincent and Ewen Park is *most nearly* _____ feet.

   A. 2,000 B. 6,000 C. 24,000 D. 12,000

COAST & GEODETIC MAP F

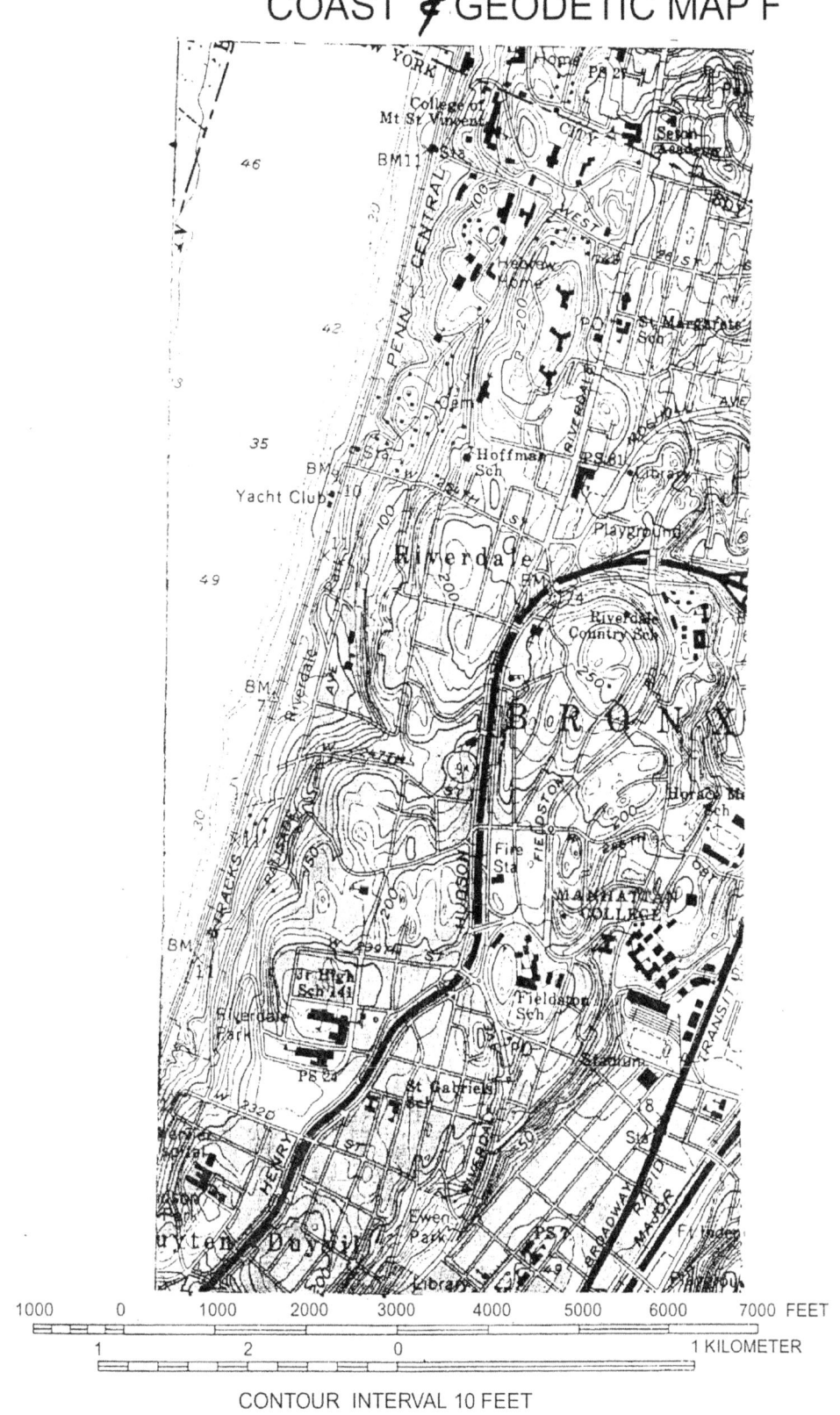

CONTOUR INTERVAL 10 FEET

KEY (CORRECT ANSWERS)

1. A
2. D

TEST 7

DIRECTIONS: Each question or incomplete statement is followed by several suggested answers or completions. Select the one that BEST answers the question or completes the statement. *PRINT THE LETTER OF THE CORRECT ANSWER IN THE SPACE AT THE RIGHT.*

Questions 1-3.

DIRECTIONS: Questions 1 to 3, inclusive, are based on information contained on Sketch G, a birds-eye view of a proposed development.

NOTE: The attached single family homes in the periphery are one-story high and contain 1,000 square feet. They are square buildings.

1. The dimension A of this single family attached home is *most nearly* _____ feet. 1._____
   A. 20   B. 32   C. 50   D. 100

2. The dimension B of the road is *most nearly* _____ feet. 2._____
   A. 25   B. 48   C. 75   D. 100

3. The dimension C of the courtyard is *most nearly* _____ feet. 3._____
   A. 40   B. 85   C. 57   D. 150

2 (#7)

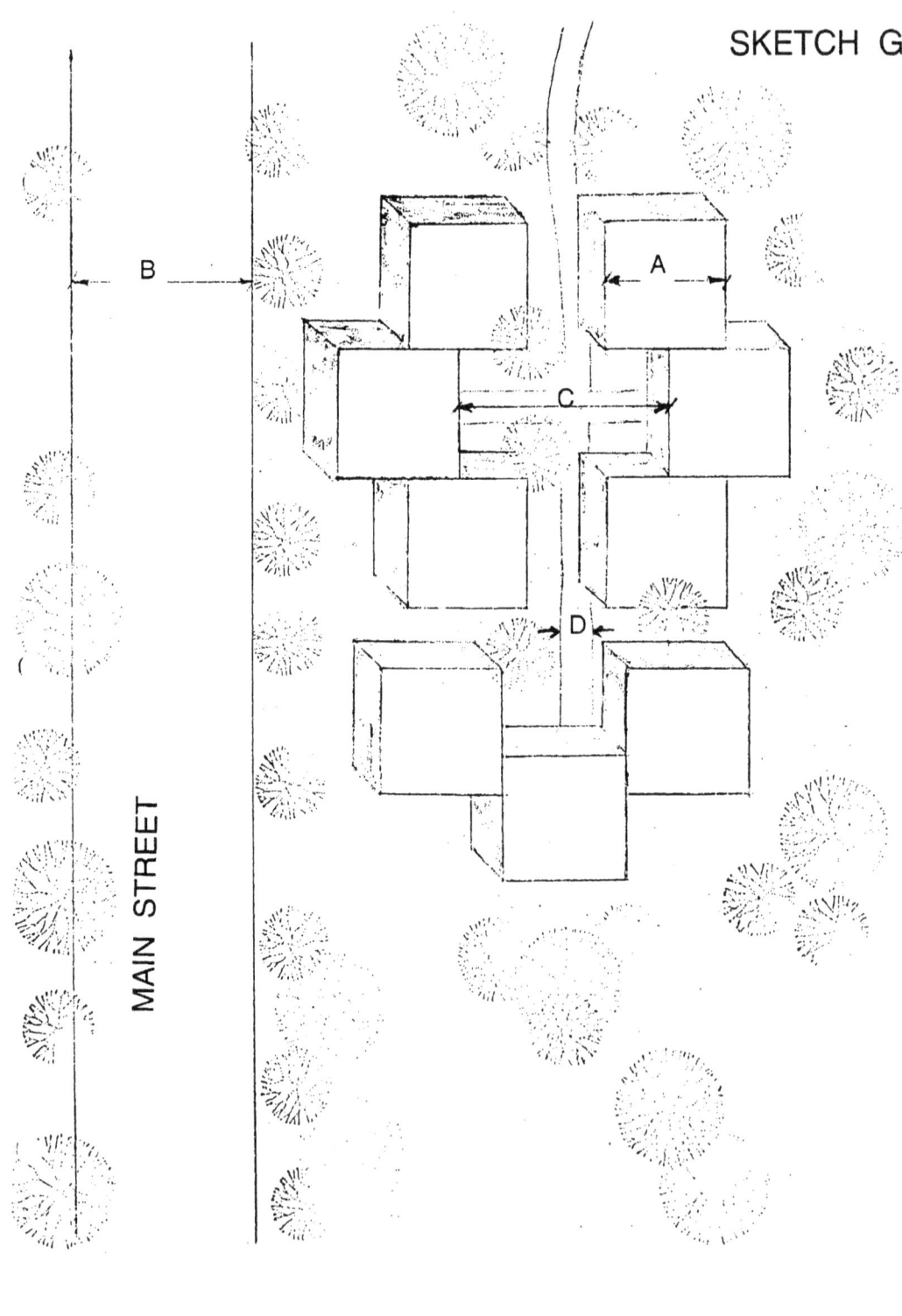

SKETCH G

KEY (CORRECT ANSWERS)

1. B
2. B
3. C

EXAMINATION SECTION
TEST 1

DIRECTIONS: Each question or incomplete statement is followed by several suggested answers or completions. Select the one that BEST answers the question or completes the statement. *PRINT THE LETTER OF THE CORRECT ANSWER IN THE SPACE AT THE RIGHT.*

1. The one of the following which is the CHIEF reason for the difference between the administration of justice agencies and that of other units in public administration is that
   A. correctional institutions are concerned with security
   B. some defendants are proven to be innocent after trial
   C. the administration of justice is more complicated than other aspects of public administration
   D. correctional institutions produce services their clients or customers fail to understand or ask for

   1.____

2. Of the following, the MOST important reason why employees resist change is that
   A. they have not received adequate training in preparation for the change
   B. experience has shown that when new ideas don't work, employees get blamed and not the individuals responsible for the new ideas
   C. new ideas and methods almost always represent a threat to the security of the individuals involved
   D. new ideas often are not practical and disrupt operations unnecessarily

   2.____

3. Stress situations are ideal for building up a backlog of knowledge about an employee's behavior. Not only does it inform the supervisor of many aspects of a person's behavior patterns, but it is also vitally important to have foreknowledge of how people behave under stress.
   The one of the following which is NOT implied by this passage is that
   A. a person under stress may give some indication of his unsuitability for work in an institution
   B. putting people under stress is the best means of determining their usual patterns of behavior
   C. stress situations may give important clues about performance in the service
   D. there is a need to know about a person's reaction to situations *when the chips are down*

   3.____

4. There are situations requiring a supervisor to give direct orders to subordinates assigned to work under the direct control of other supervisors.
   Under which of the following conditions would this shift of command responsibility be MOST appropriate?
   A. Emergency operations require the cooperative action of two or more organizational units.

   4.____

B. One of the other supervisors is not doing his job, thus defeating the goals of the organization.
C. The subordinates are performing their assigned tasks in the absence of their own supervisor.
D. The subordinates ask a superior officer who is not their own supervisor how to perform an assignment given them by their supervisor.

5. The one of the following which BEST differentiates staff supervision from line supervision is that
   A. staff supervision has the authority to immediately correct a line subordinate's action
   B. staff supervision is an advisory relationship
   C. line supervision goes beyond the normal boundaries of direct supervision within a command
   D. line supervision does not report findings and make recommendations

6. Decision-making is a rational process calling for a *suspended judgment* by the supervisor until all the facts have been ascertained and analyzed, and the consequences of alternative courses of action studied; then the decision maker
   A. acts as both judge and jury and selects what he believes to be the best of the alternative plans
   B. consults with those who will be most directly involved to obtain a recommendation as to the most appropriate course of action
   C. reviews the facts which he has already analyzed, reduces his thoughts to writing, and selects that course of action which can have the fewest negative consequences if his thinking contains an error
   D. stops, considers the matter for at least a 24-hour period, before referring it to a superior for evaluation

7. Decision-making can be defined as the
   A. delegation of authority and responsibility to persons capable of performing their assigned duties with moderate or little supervision
   B. imposition of a supervisor's decision upon a work group
   C. technique of selecting the course of action with the most desired consequences, and the least undesired or unexpected consequence
   D. process principally concerned with improvement of procedures

8. A supervisor who is not well-motivated and has no desire to accept basic responsibilities will
   A. compromise to the extent of permitting poor performance for lengthy periods without correction
   B. get good performance from his work group if the employees are satisfied with their pay and other working conditions
   C. not have marginal workers in his work group if the work is interesting
   D. perform adequately as long as the work of his group consists of routine operations

9. A supervisor is more than a bond or connecting link between two levels of employees. He has joint responsibility which must be shared with both management and with the work group.
Of the following, the item which BEST expresses the meaning of this statement is:
   A. A supervisor works with both management and the work group and must reconcile the differences between them.
   B. In management, the supervisor is solely concerned with efforts directing the work of his subordinates.
   C. The supervisory role is basically that of a liaison man between management and the work force.
   D. What a supervisor says and does when confronted with day-to-day problems depends upon is level in the organization.

9.____

10. Operations research is the observation of operations in business or government, and it utilizes both hypotheses and controlled experiments to determine the outcome of decisions. In effect, it reproduces the future impact on the decision in a clinical environment suited to intensive study.
Operations research has
   A. been more promising than applied research in the ascertaining of knowledge for the purpose of decision-making
   B. never been amenable to fact analysis on the grand scale
   C. not been used extensively in government
   D. proven to be the only rational and logical approach to decision-making on long-range problems

10.____

11. Assume that a civilian makes a complaint regarding the behavior of a certain worker to the supervisor of the worker. The supervisor regards the complaint as unjustified and unreasonable.
In this circumstances, the supervisor
   A. must make a written note of the complaint and forward it through channels to the unit or individual responsible for complaint investigations
   B. should assure the complainant that disciplinary action will be appropriate to the seriousness of the alleged offense
   C. should immediately summon the worker if he is available so that the latter may attempt to straighten out the difficulty
   D. should inform the complainant that his complaint appears to be unjustified and unreasonable

11.____

12. Modern management usually establishes a personal history folder for an employee at the time of hiring. Disciplinary matters appear in such personal history folders. Employees do not like the idea of disciplinary actions appearing in their permanent personal folders.
Authorities believe that
   A. after a few years have passed since the commission of the infraction, disciplinary actions should be removed from folders
   B. disciplinary actions should remain in folders; it is not the records but the use of records that requires detailed study

12.____

C. most personnel have not had disciplinary action taken against them and would resent the removal of disciplinary actions for such folders
D. there is no point in removing disciplinary actions from personal history folders since employees who have been guilty of infractions should not be allowed to forget their infractions

13. While supervisors should not fear the acceptance of responsibility, they
    A. generally seek out responsibility that subordinates should exercise, particularly when the supervisors do not have sufficient work to do
    B. must be on guard against the abuse of authority that often accompanies the acceptance of total responsibility
    C. should avoid responsibility that is customarily exercised by their superiors
    D. who are anxious for promotions accept responsibility but do not exercise the authority warranted by the responsibility

14. Planning is part of the decision-making process. By planning is meant the development of details of alternative plans of action.
    The key to *effective* planning is
    A. careful research to determine whether a tentative plan has been tried at some time in the past
    B. participation by employees in planning, preferably those employees who will be involved in putting the selected plan into action
    C. speed; poor plans can be discarded after they are put into effect while good plans usually are not put into effect because of delays
    D. writing the plan up in considerable detail and then forwarding the plan, through channels, to the executive officer having final approval of the plan

15. Equating strict discipline with punitive measures and lax discipline with rehabilitation creates a false dichotomy.
    The one of the statements given below that would BEST follow from the belief expressed in this statement is that discipline
    A. is important for treatment
    B. militates against treatment programs
    C. is not an important consideration in institutions where effective rehabilitation programs prevail
    D. minimizes the need for punitive measures if it is strict

16. If training starts at the lower level of command, it is like planting a seed in tilled ground but removing the sun and rain. Seeds cannot grow unless they have help from above.
    Of the following, the MOST appropriate conclusion to be drawn from this statement is that
    A. the head of an institution may not delegate authority for the planning of an institutional training program for staff
    B. on-the-job training is better than formalized training courses
    C. regularly scheduled training courses must be planned in advance
    D. staff training is the responsibility of higher levels of comman

17. The one of the following that BEST describes the meaning of *in-service staff training* is:
    A. The training of personnel who are below average in performance
    B. The training given to each employee throughout his employment
    C. The training of staff only in their own specialized fields
    D. Classroom training where the instructor and employees develop a positive and productive relationship leading to improved efficiency on the job

17.____

18. All bureau personnel should be concerned about, and involved in, public relations.
    Of the following, the MOST important reason for this statement is that
    A. an institution is an agency of the government supported by public funds and responsible to the public
    B. institutions are places of public business and, therefore, the public is interested in them
    C. some personnel need publicity in order to advance
    D. personnel sometimes need publicity in order to ensure that their grievances are acted upon by higher authority

18.____

19. The MOST important factor in establishing a disciplinary policy in an organization is
    A. consistency of application
    B. strict supervisors
    C. strong enforcement
    D. the degree of toughness or laxity

19.____

20. The FIRST step in planning a program is to
    A. clearly define the objectives
    B. estimate the costs
    C. hire a program director
    D. solicit funds

20.____

21. The PRIMARY purpose of control in an organization is to
    A. punish those who do not do their job well
    B. get people to do what is necessary to achieve an objective
    C. develop clearly stated rules and regulations
    D. regulate expenditures

21.____

22. The UNDERLYING principle of *sound* administration is to
    A. base administration on investigation of facts
    B. have plenty of resources available
    C. hire a strong administrator
    D. establish a broad policy

22.____

23. An IMPORTANT aspect to keep in mind during the decision-making process is that
    A. all possible alternatives for attaining goals should be sought out and considered
    B. considering various alternatives only leads to confusion
    C. once a decision has been made, it cannot be retracted
    D. there is only one correct method to reach any goal

23.____

24. Implementation of accountability requires
    A. a leader who will not hesitate to take punitive action
    B. an established system of communication from the bottom to the top
    C. explicit directives from leaders
    D. too much expense to justify it

25. The CHIEF danger of a decentralized control system is that
    A. excessive reports and communications will be generated
    B. problem areas may not be detected readily
    C. the expense will become prohibitive
    D. this will result in too many *chiefs*

KEY (CORRECT ANSWERS)

1.	D		11.	D
2.	C		12.	A
3.	B		13.	B
4.	A		14.	B
5.	B		15.	A
6.	A		16.	D
7.	C		17.	B
8.	A		18.	A
9.	A		19.	A
10.	C		20.	A

21.	B
22.	A
23.	A
24.	B
25.	B

TEST 2

DIRECTIONS: Each question or incomplete statement is followed by several suggested answers or completions. Select the one that BEST answers the question or completes the statement. *PRINT THE LETTER OF THE CORRECT ANSWER IN THE SPACE AT THE RIGHT.*

1. When giving orders to his subordinates, a certain supervisor often includes information as to why the work is necessary.
   This approach by the supervisor is GENERALLY
   A. *inadvisable*, since it appears that he is avoiding responsibility and wishes to blame his superiors
   B. *inadvisable*, since it creates the impression that he is trying to impress the subordinates with his importance
   C. *advisable*, since it serves to motivate the subordinates by giving them a reason for wanting to do the work
   D. *advisable*, since it shows that he is knowledgeable and is in control of his assignments

1.____

2. Some supervisors often ask capable, professional subordinates to get some work done with questions such as: *Mary, would you try to complete that work today?*
   The use of such request orders USUALLY
   A. gets results which are as good as or better than results from direct orders
   B. shows the supervisor to be weak and lowers the respect of his subordinates
   C. provokes resentment as compared to the use of direct orders
   D. leads to confusion as to the proper procedure to follow when carrying out orders

2.____

3. Assume that a supervisor, because of an emergency when time was essential, and in the absence of his immediate superior, went out of the chain of command to get a decision from a higher level.
   It would consequently be MOST appropriate for the immediate superior to
   A. reprimand him for his action, since the long-range consequences are far more detrimental than the immediate gain
   B. encourage him to use this method, since the chain of command is an outmoded and discredited system which inhibits productive work
   C. order him to refrain from any repetition of this action in the future
   D. support him as long as he informed the superior of the action at the earliest opportunity

3.____

4. A supervisor gave instructions which he knew were somewhat complex to a subordinate. He then asked the subordinate to repeat the instructions to him.
   The supervisor's decision to have the subordinate repeat the instructions was
   A. *good practice*, mainly because the subordinate would realize the importance of carefully following instructions

4.____

83

B. *poor practice*, mainly because the supervisor should have given the employee time to ponder the instructions, and then, if necessary, to ask questions
C. *good practice*, mainly because the supervisor could see whether the subordinate had any apparent problem in understanding the instructions
D. *poor practice*, mainly because the subordinate should not be expected to have the same degree of knowledge as the supervisor

5. Supervisors and subordinates must successfully communicate with each other in order to work well together.
Which of the following statements concerning communication of this type is CORRECT?
   A. When speaking to his subordinates, a supervisor should make every effort to appear knowledgeable about all aspects of their work.
   B. Written communications should be prepared by the supervisor at his own level of comprehension.
   C. The average employee tends to give meaning to communication according to his personal interpretation.
   D. The effective supervisor communicates as much information as he has available to anyone who is interested.

5.____

6. A supervisor should be aware of situations in which it is helpful to put his orders to his subordinates in writing.
Which of the following situations would MOST likely call for a written order rather than an oral order?
The order
   A. gives complicated instructions which vary from ordinary practice
   B. involves the performance of duties for which the subordinate is responsible
   C. directs subordinates to perform duties similar to those which they performed in the recent past
   D. concerns a matter that must be promptly completed or dealt with

6.____

7. Assume that a supervisor discovers that a false rumor about possible layoffs has spread among his subordinates through the grapevine.
Of the following, the BEST way for the supervisor to deal with this situation is to
   A. use the grapevine to leak accurate information
   B. call a meeting to provide information and to answer questions
   C. post a notice on the bulletin board denying the rumor
   D. institute procedures designed to eliminate the grapevine

7.____

8. Communications in an organization with many levels becomes subject to different interpretations at each level and have a tendency to become distorted. The more levels there are in an organization, the greater the likelihood that the final recipient of a communication will get the wrong message.
The one of the following statements which BEST supports the foregoing viewpoint is:
   A. Substantial communications problems exist at high management levels in organizations.

8.____

B. There is a relationship in an organization between the number of hierarchical levels and interference with communications.
C. An opportunity should be given to subordinates at all levels to communicate their views with impunity.
D. In larger organizations, there tends to be more interference with downward communications than with upward communications.

9. A subordinate comes to you, his supervisor, to ask a detailed question about a new agency directive; however, you do not know the answer.
Of the following, the MOST helpful response to give the subordinate is to
   A. point out that since your own supervisor has failed to keep you informed of this matter, it is probably unimportant
   B. give the most logical interpretation you can, based on your best judgment
   C. ask him to raise the question with other supervisors until he finds one who knows the answer, then let you know also
   D. explain that you do not know and assure him that you will get the information for him

10. The traditional view of management theory is that communication in an organization should follow the table of organization. A newer theory holds that timely communication often requires bypassing certain steps in the hierarchical chain.
However, the MAIN advantage of using formal channels of communication within an organization is that
   A. an employee is thereby restricted in his relationships to his immediate superior and his immediate subordinates
   B. information is thereby transmitted to everyone who should be informed
   C. the organization will have an appeal channel, or a mechanism by which subordinates can go over their superior's head
   D. employees are thereby encouraged to exercise individual initiative

11. It is unfair to hold subordinates responsible for the performance of duties for which they do not have the requisite authority.
When this is done, it violates the principle that
   A. responsibility cannot be greater than that implied by delegated authority
   B. responsibility should be greater than that implied by delegated authority
   C. authority cannot be greater than that implied by delegated responsibility
   D. authority should be greater than that implied by delegated responsibility

12. Assume that a supervisor wishes to delegate some tasks to a capable subordinate.
It would be MOST in keeping with the principles of delegation for the supervisor to
   A. ask another supervisor who is experienced in the delegated tasks to evaluate the subordinate's work from time to time
   B. monitor continually the subordinate's performance by carefully reviewing his work

4 (#2)

C. request experienced employees to submit peer ratings of the work of the subordinate
D. tell the subordinates what problems are likely to be encountered and specify which problems to report on

13. There are three types of leadership: *autocratic*, in which the leader makes the decisions and seeks compliance from his subordinates; *democratic*, in which the leader consults with his subordinate and lets them help set policy; and *free rein*, in which the leader acts as an information center and exercises minimum control over his subordinates.
A supervisor can be MOST effective if he decides to
    A. use democratic leadership techniques exclusively
    B. avoid the use of autocratic leadership techniques entirely
    C. employ the three types of leadership according to the situation
    D. rely mainly on autocratic leadership techniques

13.____

14. During a busy period of work, Employee A asked his supervisor for leave in order to take an ordinary vacation. The supervisor denied the request. The following day, Employee B asked for leave during the same period because his wife had just gone to the hospital for an indeterminate stay and he had family matters to tend to.
Of the following, the BEST way for the supervisor to deal with Employee B's request is to
    A. grant the request and give the reason to the other employee
    B. suggest that the employee make his request to higher management
    C. delay the request immediately since granting it would show favoritism
    D. defer any decision until the duration of the hospital stay is determined

14.____

15. Assume that you are a supervisor and that a subordinate tells you he has a grievance.
In general, you should FIRST
    A. move the grievance forward in order to get a prompt decision
    B. discourage this type of behavior on the part of subordinates
    C. attempt to settle the grievance
    D. refer the subordinate to the personnel office

15.____

16. A supervisor may have available a large variety of rewards he can use to motivate his subordinates. However, some supervisors choose the wrong rewards.
A supervisor is MOST likely to make such a mistake if he
    A. appeals to a subordinate's desire to be well regarded by his co-workers
    B. assumes that the subordinate's goals and preferences are the same as his own
    C. conducts in-depth discussions with a subordinate in order to discover his preference
    D. limits incentives to those rewards which he is authorized to provide or to recommend

16.____

17. Employee performance appraisal is open to many kinds of errors. When a supervisor is preparing such an appraisal, he is MOST likely to commit an error if
    A. employees are indifferent to the consequences of their performance appraisals
    B. the entire period for which the evaluation is being made is taken into consideration
    C. standard measurement criteria are used as performance benchmarks
    D. personal characteristics of employees which are not job-related are given weight

18. Assume that a supervisor finds that a report prepared by an employee is unsatisfactory and should be done over.
    Which of the following should the supervisor do?
    A. Give the report to another employee who can complete it properly
    B. Have the report done over by the same employee after successfully training him
    C. Hold a meeting to train all the employees so as not to single out the employee who performed unsatisfactory
    D. Accept the report so as not to discourage the employee and then make the corrections himself

19. Employees sometimes wish to have personal advice and counseling, in confidence, about their job-related problems. These problems may include such concerns as health matters, family difficulties, alcoholism, debts, emotional disturbances, etc.
    Such assistance is BEST provided through
    A. maintenance of an exit interview program to find reasons for, and solutions to, turn-over problems
    B. arrangements for employees to discuss individual problems informally outside normal administrative channels
    C. procedures which allow employees to submit anonymous inquiries to the personnel department
    D. special hearing committees consisting of top management in addition to immediate supervisors

20. An employee is always a member of some unit of the formal organization. He may also be a member of an informal work group.
    With respect to employee productivity and job satisfaction, the informal work group can MOST accurately be said to
    A. have no influence of any kind on its members
    B. influence its members negatively only
    C. influence its members positively only
    D. influence its members negatively or positively

21. In order to encourage employees to make suggestions, many public agencies have employee suggestion programs.
    What is the MAJOR benefit of such a program to the agency as a whole?

It
- A. brings existing or future problems to management's attention
- B. reduces the number of minor accidents
- C. requires employees to share in decision-making responsibilities
- D. reveals employees who have inadequate job knowledge

22. Assume that you have been asked to interview a seemingly shy applicant for a temporary position in your department.
For you to ask the kinds of questions that begin with *What, Where, Why, When, Who,* and *How,* is
    - A. *good practice*; it informs the applicant that he must conform to the requirements of the department
    - B. *poor practice*; it exceeds the extent and purpose of an initial interview
    - C. *good practice*; it encourages the applicant to talk to a greater extent
    - D. *poor practice*; it encourages the applicant to dominate the discussion

23. In recent years, job enlargement or job enrichment has tended to replace job simplification.
Those who advocate job enrichment or enlargement consider it *desirable* CHIEFLY because
    - A. it allows supervisors to control closely the activities of subordinates
    - B. it produces greater job satisfaction through reduction of responsibility
    - C. most employees prefer to avoid work which is new and challenging
    - D. positions with routinized duties are unlikely to provide job satisfaction

24. Job rotation is a training method in which an employee temporarily changes places with another employee of equal rank.
What is usually the MAIN purpose of job rotation? To
    - A. politely remove the person being rotated from an unsuitable assignment
    - B. increase skills and provide broader experience
    - C. prepare the person being rotated for a permanent change
    - D. test the skills of the person being rotated

25. There are several principles that a supervisor needs to know if he is to deal adequately with his training responsibilities.
Which of the following is usually NOT a principle of training?
    - A. People should be trained according to their individual needs.
    - B. People can learn by being told or shown how to do work but best of all by doing work under guidance.
    - C. People can be easily trained even if they have no desire to learn.
    - D. Training should be planned, scheduled, executed, and evaluated systematically.

KEY (CORRECT ANSWERS)

1.	C	11.	A
2.	A	12.	D
3.	D	13.	C
4.	C	14.	A
5.	C	15.	C
6.	A	16.	B
7.	B	17.	D
8.	B	18.	B
9.	D	19.	B
10.	B	20.	D

21. A
22. C
23. D
24. B
25. C

PHILOSOPHY, PRINCIPLES, PRACTICES, AND TECHNICS
OF
SUPERVISION, ADMINISTRATION, MANAGEMENT, AND ORGANIZATION

TABLE OF CONTENTS

	Page
MEANING OF SUPERVISION	1
THE OLD AND THE NEW SUPERVISION	1
THE EIGHT (8) BASIC PRINCIPLES OF THE NEW SUPERVISION	1
I. Principle of Responsibility	1
II. Principle of Authority	2
III. Principle of Self-Growth	2
IV. Principle of Individual Worth	2
V. Principle of Creative Leadership	2
VI. Principle of Success and Failure	2
VII. Principle of Science	3
VIII. Principle of Cooperation	3
WHAT IS ADMINISTRATION?	3
I. Practices Commonly Classed as "Supervisory"	3
II. Practices Commonly Classed as "Administrative"	3
III. Practices Commonly Classed as Both "Supervisory" and "Administrative"	4
RESPONSIBILITIES OF THE SUPERVISOR	4
COMPETENCIES OF THE SUPERVISOR	4
THE PROFESSIONAL SUPERVISOR-EMPLOYEE RELATIONSHIP	4
MINI-TEXT IN SUPERVISION, ADMINISTRATION, MANAGEMENT, AND ORGANIZATION	5
I. Brief Highlights	5
A. Levels of Management	6
B. What the Supervisor Must Learn	6
C. A Definition of Supervision	6
D. Elements of the Team Concept	6
E. Principles of Organization	6
F. The Four Important Parts of Every Job	7
G. Principles of Delegation	7
H. Principles of Effective Communications	7
I. Principles of Work Improvement	7
J. Areas of Job Improvement	7
K. Seven Key Points in Making Improvements	8

	L.	Corrective Techniques for Job Improvement	8
	M.	A Planning Checklist	8
	N.	Five Characteristics of Good Directions	9
	O.	Types of Directions	9
	P.	Controls	9
	Q.	Orienting the New Employee	9
	R.	Checklist for Orienting New Employees	9
	S.	Principles of Learning	10
	T.	Causes of Poor Performance	10
	U.	Four Major Steps in On-the-Job Instructions	10
	V.	Employees Want Five Things	10
	W.	Some Don'ts in Regard to Praise	11
	X.	How to Gain Your Workers' Confidence	11
	Y.	Sources of Employee Problems	11
	Z.	The Supervisor's Key to Discipline	11
	AA.	Five Important Processes of Management	12
	BB.	When the Supervisor Fails to Plan	12
	CC.	Fourteen General Principles of Management	12
	DD.	Change	12
II.	Brief Topical Summaries		13
	A.	Who/What is the Supervisor?	13
	B.	The Sociology of Work	13
	C.	Principles and Practices of Supervision	14
	D.	Dynamic Leadership	14
	E.	Processes for Solving Problems	15
	F.	Training for Results	15
	G.	Health, Safety, and Accident Prevention	16
	H.	Equal Employment Opportunity	16
	I.	Improving Communications	16
	J.	Self-Development	17
	K.	Teaching and Training	17
		1. The Teaching Process	17
		a. Preparation	17
		b. Presentation	18
		c. Summary	18
		d. Application	18
		e. Evaluation	18
		2. Teaching Methods	18
		a. Lecture	18
		b. Discussion	18
		c. Demonstration	19
		d. Performance	19
		e. Which Method to Use	19

PHILOSOPHY, PRINCIPLES, PRACTICES, AND TECHNICS
OF
SUPERVISION, ADMINISTRATION, MANAGEMENT, AND ORGANIZATION

MEANING OF SUPERVISION

The extension of the democratic philosophy has been accompanied by an extension in the scope of supervision. Modern leaders and supervisors no longer think of supervision in the narrow sense of being confined chiefly to visiting employees, supplying materials, or rating the staff. They regard supervision as being intimately related to all the concerned agencies of society, they speak of the supervisor's function in terms of "growth," rather than the "improvement" of employees.

This modern concept of supervision may be defined as follows: Supervision is leadership and the development of leadership within groups which are cooperatively engaged in inspection, research, training, guidance, and evaluation.

THE OLD AND THE NEW SUPERVISION

TRADITIONAL
1. Inspection
2. Focused on the employee
3. Visitation
4. Random and haphazard
5. Imposed and authoritarian
6. One person usually

MODERN
1. Study and analysis
2. Focused on aims, materials, methods, supervisors, employees, environment
3. Demonstrations, intervisitation, workshops, directed reading, bulletins, etc.
4. Definitely organized and planned (scientific)
5. Cooperative and democratic
6. Many persons involved (creative)

THE EIGHT (8) BASIC PRINCIPLES OF THE NEW SUPERVISION

I. Principle of Responsibility
    Authority to act and responsibility for acting must be joined.
    A. If you give responsibility, give authority.
    B. Define employee duties clearly.
    C. Protect employees from criticism by others.
    D. Recognize the rights as well as obligations of employees.
    E. Achieve the aims of a democratic society insofar as it is possible within the area of your work.
    F. Establish a situation favorable to training and learning.
    G. Accept ultimate responsibility for everything done in your section, unit, office, division, department.
    H. Good administration and good supervision are inseparable.

II. Principle of Authority
The success of the supervisor is measured by the extent to which the power of authority is not used.
   A. Exercise simplicity and informality in supervision
   B. Use the simplest machinery of supervision
   C. If it is good for the organization as a whole, it is probably justified.
   D. Seldom be arbitrary or authoritative.
   E. Do not base your work on the power of position or of personality.
   F. Permit and encourage the free expression of opinions.

III. Principle of Self-Growth
The success of the supervisor is measured by the extent to which, and the speed with which, he is no longer needed.
   A. Base criticism on principles, not on specifics.
   B. Point out higher activities to employees.
   C. Train for self-thinking by employees to meet new situations.
   D. Stimulate initiative, self-reliance, and individual responsibility
   E. Concentrate on stimulating the growth of employees rather than on removing defects.

IV. Principle of Individual Worth
Respect for the individual is a paramount consideration in supervision.
   A. Be human and sympathetic in dealing with employees.
   B. Don't nag about things to be done.
   C. Recognize the individual differences among employees and seek opportunities to permit best expression of each personality.

V. Principle of Creative Leadership
The best supervision is that which is not apparent to the employee.
   A. Stimulate, don't drive employees to creative action.
   B. Emphasize doing good things.
   C. Encourage employees to do what they do best.
   D. Do not be too greatly concerned with details of subject or method.
   E. Do not be concerned exclusively with immediate problems and activities.
   F. Reveal higher activities and make them both desired and maximally possible.
   G. Determine procedures in the light of each situation but see that these are derived from a sound basic philosophy.
   H. Aid, inspire, and lead so as to liberate the creative spirit latent in all good employees.

VI. Principle of Success and Failure
There are no unsuccessful employees, only unsuccessful supervisors who have failed to give proper leadership.
   A. Adapt suggestions to the capacities, attitudes, and prejudices of employees.
   B. Be gradual, be progressive, be persistent.
   C. Help the employee find the general principle; have the employee apply his own problem to the general principle.
   D. Give adequate appreciation for good work and honest effort.
   E. Anticipate employee difficulties and help to prevent them.
   F. Encourage employees to do the desirable things they will do anyway.
   G. Judge your supervision by the results it secures.

VII. Principle of Science
Successful supervision is scientific, objective, and experimental. It is based on facts, not on prejudices.
   A. Be cumulative in results.
   B. Never divorce your suggestions from the goals of training.
   C. Don't be impatient of results.
   D. Keep all matters on a professional, not a personal, level.
   E. Do not be concerned exclusively with immediate problems and activities.
   F. Use objective means of determining achievement and rating where possible.

VIII. Principle of Cooperation
Supervision is a cooperative enterprise between supervisor and employee.
   A. Begin with conditions as they are.
   B. Ask opinions of all involved when formulating policies.
   C. Organization is as good as its weakest link.
   D. Let employees help to determine policies and department programs.
   E. Be approachable and accessible—physically and mentally.
   F. Develop pleasant social relationships.

WHAT IS ADMINISTRATION

Administration is concerned with providing the environment, the material facilities, and the operational procedures that will promote the maximum growth and development of supervisors and employees. (Organization is an aspect and a concomitant of administration.)

There is no sharp line of demarcation between supervision and administration; these functions are intimately interrelated and, often, overlapping. They are complementary activities.

I. Practices Commonly Classed as "Supervisory"
   A. Conducting employees' conferences
   B. Visiting sections, units, offices, divisions, departments
   C. Arranging for demonstrations
   D. Examining plans
   E. Suggesting professional reading
   F. Interpreting bulletins
   G. Recommending in-service training courses
   H. Encouraging experimentation
   I. Appraising employee morale
   J. Providing for intervisitation

II. Practices Commonly Classified as "Administrative"
   A. Management of the office
   B. Arrangement of schedules for extra duties
   C. Assignment of rooms or areas
   D. Distribution of supplies
   E. Keeping records and reports
   F. Care of audio-visual materials
   G. Keeping inventory records
   H. Checking record cards and books

I. Programming special activities
J. Checking on the attendance and punctuality of employees

III. Practices Commonly Classified as Both "Supervisory" and "Administrative"
   A. Program construction
   B. Testing or evaluating outcomes
   C. Personnel accounting
   D. Ordering instructional materials

RESPONSIBILITIES OF THE SUPERVISOR

A person employed in a supervisory capacity must constantly be able to improve his own efficiency and ability. He represent the employer to the employees and only continuous self-examination can make him a capable supervisor.

Leadership and training are the supervisor's responsibility. An efficient working unit is one in which the employees work with the supervisor. It is his job to bring out the best in his employees. He must always be relaxed, courteous, and calm in his association with his employees. Their feelings are important, and a harsh attitude does not develop the most efficient employees.

COMPETENCES OF THE SUPERVISOR

I. Complete knowledge of the duties and responsibilities of his position.
II. To be able to organize a job, plan ahead, and carry through.
III. To have self-confidence and initiative.
IV. To be able to handle the unexpected situation and make quick decisions.
V. To be able to properly train subordinates in the positions they are best suited for.
VI. To be able to keep good human relations among his subordinates.
VII. To be able to keep good human relations between his subordinates and himself and to earn their respect and trust.

THE PROFESSIONAL SUPERVISOR-EMPLOYEE RELATIONSHIP

There are two kinds of efficiency: one kind is only apparent and is produced in organizations through the exercise of mere discipline; this is but a simulation of the second, or true, efficiency which springs from spontaneous cooperation. If you are a manager, no matter how great or small your responsibility, it is your job, in the final analysis, to create and develop this involuntary cooperation among the people whom you supervise. For, no matter how powerful a combination of money, machines, and materials a company may have, this is a dead and sterile thing without a team of willing, thinking, and articulate people to guide it.

The following 21 points are presented as indicative of the exemplary basic relationship that should exist between supervisor and employee:

1. Each person wants to be liked and respected by his fellow employee and wants to be treated with consideration and respect by his superior.
2. The most competent employee will make an error. However, in a unit where good relations exist between the supervisor and his employees, tenseness and fear do not exist. Thus, errors are not hidden or covered up, and the efficiency of a unit is not impaired.

3. Subordinates resent rules, regulations, or orders that are unreasonable or unexplained.
4. Subordinates are quick to resent unfairness, harshness, injustices, and favoritism.
5. An employee will accept responsibility if he knows that he will be complimented for a job well done, and not too harshly chastised for failure; that his supervisor will check the cause of the failure, and, if it was the supervisor's fault, he will assume the blame therefore. If it was the employee's fault, his supervisor will explain the correct method or means of handling the responsibility.
6. An employee wants to receive credit for a suggestion he has made, that is used. If a suggestion cannot be used, the employee is entitled to an explanation. The supervisor should not say "no" and close the subject.
7. Fear and worry slow up a worker's ability. Poor working environment can impair his physical and mental health. A good supervisor avoids forceful methods, threats, and arguments to get a job done.
8. A forceful supervisor is able to train his employees individually and as a team, and is able to motivate them in the proper channels.
9. A mature supervisor is able to properly evaluate his subordinates and to keep them happy and satisfied.
10. A sensitive supervisor will never patronize his subordinates.
11. A worthy supervisor will respect his employees' confidences.
12. Definite and clear-cut responsibilities should be assigned to each executive.
13. Responsibility should always be coupled with corresponding authority.
14. No change should be made in the scope or responsibilities of a position without a definite understanding to that effect on the part of all persons concerned.
15. No executive or employee, occupying a single position in the organization, should be subject to definite orders from more than one source.
16. Orders should never be given to subordinates over the head of a responsible executive. Rather than do this, the officer in question should be supplanted.
17. Criticisms of subordinates should, whoever possible, be made privately, and in no case should a subordinate be criticized in the presence of executives or employees of equal or lower rank.
18. No dispute or difference between executives or employees as to authority or responsibilities should be considered too trivial for prompt and careful adjudication.
19. Promotions, wage changes, and disciplinary action should always be approved by the executive immediately superior to the one directly responsible.
20. No executive or employee should ever be required, or expected, to be at the same time an assistant to, and critic of, another.
21. Any executive whose work is subject to regular inspection should, wherever practicable, be given the assistance and facilities necessary to enable him to maintain an independent check of the quality of his work.

MINI-TEXT IN SUPERVISION, ADMINISTRATION, MANAGEMENT, AND ORGANIZATION

I. Brief Highlights

Listed concisely and sequentially are major headings and important data in the field for quick recall and review.

A. Levels of Management
Any organization of some size has several levels of management. In terms of a ladder, the levels are:

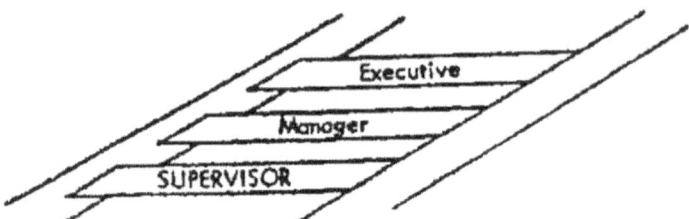

The first level is very important because it is the beginning point of management leadership.

B. What the Supervisor Must Learn
A supervisor must learn to:
1. Deal with people and their differences
2. Get the job done through people
3. Recognize the problems when they exist
4. Overcome obstacles to good performance
5. Evaluate the performance of people
6. Check his own performance in terms of accomplishment

C. A Definition of Supervisor
The term supervisor means any individual having authority, in the interests of the employer, to hire, transfer, suspend, lay-off, recall, promote, discharge, assign, reward, or discipline other employees or responsibility to direct them, or to adjust their grievances, or effectively to recommend such action, if, in connection with the foregoing, exercise of such authority is not of a merely routine or clerical nature but requires the use of independent judgment.

D. Elements of the Team Concept
What is involved in teamwork? The component parts are:
1. Members
2. A leader
3. Goals
4. Plans
5. Cooperation
6. Spirit

E. Principles of Organization
1. A team member must know what his job is.
2. Be sure that the nature and scope of a job are understood.
3. Authority and responsibility should be carefully spelled out.
4. A supervisor should be permitted to make the maximum number of decisions affecting his employees.
5. Employees should report to only one supervisor.
6. A supervisor should direct only as many employees as he can handle effectively.
7. An organization plan should be flexible.

8. Inspection and performance of work should be separate.
9. Organizational problems should receive immediate attention.
10. Assign work in line with ability and experience.

F. The Four Important Parts of Every Job
1. Inherent in every job is the *accountability* for results.
2. A second set of factors in every job is *responsibilities*.
3. Along with duties and responsibilities one must have the *authority* to act within certain limits without obtaining permission to proceed.
4. No job exists in a vacuum. The supervisor is surrounded by key *relationships*.

G. Principles of Delegation
Where work is delegated for the first time, the supervisor should think in terms of these questions:
1. Who is best qualified to do this?
2. Can an employee improve his abilities by doing this?
3. How long should an employee spend on this?
4. Are there any special problems for which he will need guidance?
5. How broad a delegation can I make?

H. Principles of Effective Communications
1. Determine the media.
2. To whom directed?
3. Identification and source authority.
4. Is communication understood?

I. Principles of Work Improvement
1. Most people usually do only the work which is assigned to them.
2. Workers are likely to fit assigned work into the time available to perform it.
3. A good workload usually stimulates output.
4. People usually do their best work when they know that results will be reviewed or inspected.
5. Employees usually feel that someone else is responsible for conditions of work, workplace layout, job methods, type of tools/equipment, and other such factors.
6. Employees are usually defensive about their job security.
7. Employees have natural resistance to change.
8. Employees can support or destroy a supervisor.
9. A supervisor usually earns the respect of his people through his personal example of diligence and efficiency.

J. Areas of Job Improvement
The areas of job improvement are quite numerous, but the most common ones which a supervisor can identify and utilize are:
1. Departmental layout
2. Flow of work
3. Workplace layout
4. Utilization of manpower
5. Work methods
6. Materials handling

7. Utilization
8. Motion economy

K. Seven Key Points in Making Improvements
1. Select the job to be improved
2. Study how it is being done now
3. Question the present method
4. Determine actions to be taken
5. Chart proposed method
6. Get approval and apply
7. Solicit worker participation

l. Corrective Techniques of Job Improvement
Specific Problems
1. Size of workload
2. Inability to meet schedules
3. Strain and fatigue
4. Improper use of men and skills
5. Waste, poor quality, unsafe conditions
6. Bottleneck conditions that hinder output
7. Poor utilization of equipment and machine
8. Efficiency and productivity of labor

General Improvement
1. Departmental layout
2. Flow of work
3. Work plan layout
4. Utilization of manpower
5. Work methods
6. Materials handling
7. Utilization of equipment
8. Motion economy

Corrective Techniques
1. Study with scale model
2. Flow chart study
3. Motion analysis
4. Comparison of units produced to standard allowance
5. Methods analysis
6. Flow chart and equipment study
7. Down time vs. running time
8. Motion analysis

M. A Planning Checklist
1. Objectives
2. Controls
3. Delegations
4. Communications
5. Resources
6. Manpower

7. Equipment
8. Supplies and materials
9. Utilization of time
10. Safety
11. Money
12. Work
13. Timing of improvements

N. Five Characteristics of Good Directions
In order to get results, directions must be:
1. Possible of accomplishment
2. Agreeable with worker interests
3. Related to mission
4. Planned and complete
5. Unmistakably clear

O. Types of Directions
1. Demands or direct orders
2. Requests
3. Suggestion or implication
4. volunteering

P. Controls
A typical listing of the overall areas in which the supervisor should establish controls might be:
1. Manpower
2. Materials
3. Quality of work
4. Quantity of work
5. Time
6. Space
7. Money
8. Methods

Q. Orienting the New Employee
1. Prepare for him
2. Welcome the new employee
3. Orientation for the job
4. Follow-up

R. Checklist for Orienting New Employees   Yes   No
1. Do you appreciate the feelings of new employees
   when they first report for work?   ___   ___
2. Are you aware of the fact that the new employee must
   make a big adjustment to his job?   ___   ___
3. Have you given him good reasons for liking the job and
   the organization?   ___   ___
4. Have you prepared for his first day on the job?   ___   ___
5. Did you welcome him cordially and make him feel needed?   ___   ___

		Yes	No
6.	Did you establish rapport with him so that he feels free to talk and discuss matters with you?	___	___
7.	Did you explain his job to him and his relationship to you?	___	___
8.	Does he know that his work will be evaluated periodically on a basis that is fair and objective?	___	___
9.	Did you introduce him to his fellow workers in such a way that they are likely to accept him?	___	___
10.	Does he know what employee benefits he will receive?	___	___
11.	Does he understand the importance of being on the job and what to do if he must leave his duty station?	___	___
12.	Has he been impressed with the importance of accident prevention and safe practice?	___	___
13.	Does he generally know his way around the department?	___	___
14.	Is he under the guidance of a sponsor who will teach the right way of doing things?	___	___
15.	Do you plan to follow-up so that he will continue to adjust successfully to his job?	___	___

S. Principles of Learning
1. Motivation
2. Demonstration or explanation
3. Practice

T. Causes of Poor Performance
1. Improper training for job
2. Wrong tools
3. Inadequate directions
4. Lack of supervisory follow-up
5. Poor communications
6. Lack of standards of performance
7. Wrong work habits
8. Low morale
9. Other

U. Four Major Steps in On-The-Job Instruction
1. Prepare the worker
2. Present the operation
3. Tryout performance
4. Follow-up

V. Employees Want Five Things
1. Security
2. Opportunity
3. Recognition
4. Inclusion
5. Expression

W. Some Don'ts in Regard to Praise
1. Don't praise a person for something he hasn't done.
2. Don't praise a person unless you can be sincere.
3. Don't be sparing in praise just because your superior withholds it from you.
4. Don't let too much time elapse between good performance and recognition of it

X. How to Gain Your Workers' Confidence
Methods of developing confidence include such things as:
1. Knowing the interests, habits, hobbies of employees
2. Admitting your own inadequacies
3. Sharing and telling of confidence in others
4. Supporting people when they are in trouble
5. Delegating matters that can be well handled
6. Being frank and straightforward about problems and working conditions
7. Encouraging others to bring their problems to you
8. Taking action on problems which impede worker progress

Y. Sources of Employee Problems
On-the-job causes might be such things as:
1. A feeling that favoritism is exercised in assignments
2. Assignment of overtime
3. An undue amount of supervision
4. Changing methods or systems
5. Stealing of ideas or trade secrets
6. Lack of interest in job
7. Threat of reduction in force
8. Ignorance or lack of communications
9. Poor equipment
10. Lack of knowing how supervisor feels toward employee
11. Shift assignments

Off-the-job problems might have to do with:
1. Health
2. Finances
3. Housing
4. Family

Z. The Supervisor's Key to Discipline
There are several key points about discipline which the supervisor should keep in mind:
1. Job discipline is one of the disciplines of life and is directed by the supervisor.
2. It is more important to correct an employee fault than to fix blame for it.
3. Employee performance is affected by problems both on the job and off.
4. Sudden or abrupt changes in behavior can be indications of important employee problems.
5. Problems should be dealt with as soon as possible after they are identified.
6. The attitude of the supervisor may have more to do with solving problems than the techniques of problem solving.
7. Correction of employee behavior should be resorted to only after the supervisor is sure that training or counseling will not be helpful.

8. Be sure to document your disciplinary actions.
9. Make sure that you are disciplining on the basis of facts rather than personal feelings.
10. Take each disciplinary step in order, being careful not to make snap judgments, or decisions based on impatience.

AA. Five Important Processes of Management
1. Planning
2. Organizing
3. Scheduling
4. Controlling
5. Motivating

BB. When the Supervisor Fails to Plan
1. Supervisor creates impression of not knowing his job
2. May lead to excessive overtime
3. Job runs itself—supervisor lacks control
4. Deadlines and appointments missed
5. Parts of the work go undone
6. Work interrupted by emergencies
7. Sets a bad example
8. Uneven workload creates peaks and valleys
9. Too much time on minor details at expense of more important tasks

CC. Fourteen General Principles of Management
1. Division of work
2. Authority and responsibility
3. Discipline
4. Unity of command
5. Unity of direction
6. Subordination of individual interest to general interest
7. Remuneration of personnel
8. Centralization
9. Scalar chain
10. Order
11. Equity
12. Stability of tenure of personnel
13. Initiative
14. Esprit de corps

DD. Change

Bringing about change is perhaps attempted more often, and yet less well understood, than anything else the supervisor does. How do people generally react to change? (People tend to resist change that is imposed upon them by other individuals or circumstances.

Change is characteristic of every situation. It is a part of every real endeavor where the efforts of people are concerned.

1. Why do people resist change?
   People may resist change because of:
   a. Fear of the unknown
   b. Implied criticism
   c. Unpleasant experiences in the past
   d. Fear of loss of status
   e. Threat to the ego
   f. Fear of loss of economic stability

2. How can we best overcome the resistance to change?
   In initiating change, take these steps:
   a. Get ready to sell
   b. Identify sources of help
   c. Anticipate objections
   d. Sell benefits
   e. Listen in depth
   f. Follow up

II. Brief Topical Summaries

   A. Who/What is the Supervisor?
   1. The supervisor is often called the "highest level employee and the lowest level manager."
   2. A supervisor is a member of both management and the work group. He acts as a bridge between the two.
   3. Most problems in supervision are in the area of human relations, or people problems.
   4. Employees expect: Respect, opportunity to learn and to advance, and a sense of belonging, and so forth.
   5. Supervisors are responsible for directing people and organizing work. Planning is of paramount importance.
   6. A position description is a set of duties and responsibilities inherent to a given position.
   7. It is important to keep the position description up-to-date and to provide each employee with his own copy.

   B. The Sociology of Work
   1. People are alike in many ways; however, each individual is unique.
   2. The supervisor is challenged in getting to know employee differences. Acquiring skills in evaluating individuals is an asset.
   3. Maintaining meaningful working relationships in the organization is of great importance.
   4. The supervisor has an obligation to help individuals to develop to their fullest potential.
   5. Job rotation on a planned basis helps to build versatility and to maintain interest and enthusiasm in work groups.
   6. Cross training (job rotation) provides backup skills.

7. The supervisor can help reduce tension by maintaining a sense of humor, providing guidance to employees, and by making reasonable and timely decisions. Employees respond favorably to working under reasonably predictable circumstances.
8. Change is characteristic of all managerial behavior. The supervisor must adjust to changes in procedures, new methods, technological changes, and to a number of new and sometimes challenging situations.
9. To overcome the natural tendency for people to resist change, the supervisor should become more skillful in initiating change.

C. Principles and Practices of Supervision
1. Employees should be required to answer to only one superior.
2. A supervisor can effectively direct only a limited number of employees, depending upon the complexity, variety, and proximity of the jobs involved.
3. The organizational chart presents the organization in graphic form. It reflects lines of authority and responsibility as well as interrelationships of units within the organization.
4. Distribution of work can be improved through an analysis using the "Work Distribution Chart."
5. The "Work Distribution Chart" reflects the division of work within a unit in understandable form.
6. When related tasks are given to an employee, he has a better chance of increasing his skills through training.
7. The individual who is given the responsibility for tasks must also be given the appropriate authority to insure adequate results.
8. The supervisor should delegate repetitive, routine work. Preparation of recurring reports, maintaining leave and attendance records are some examples.
9. Good discipline is essential to good task performance. Discipline is reflected in the actions of employees on the job in the absence of supervision.
10. Disciplinary action may have to be taken when the positive aspects of discipline have failed. Reprimand, warning, and suspension are examples of disciplinary action.
11. If a situation calls for a reprimand, be sure it is deserved and remember it is to be done in private.

D. Dynamic Leadership
1. A style is a personal method or manner of exerting influence.
2. Authoritarian leaders often see themselves as the source of power and authority.
3. The democratic leader often perceives the group as the source of authority and power.
4. Supervisors tend to do better when using the pattern of leadership that is most natural for them.
5. Social scientists suggest that the effective supervisor use the leadership style that best fits the problem or circumstances involved.
6. All four styles—telling, selling, consulting, joining—have their place. Using one does not preclude using the other at another time.

7. The theory X point of view assumes that the average person dislikes work, will avoid it whenever possible, and must be coerced to achieve organizational objectives.
8. The theory Y point of view assumes that the average person considers work to be a natural as play, and, when the individual is committed, he requires little supervision or direction to accomplish desired objectives.
9. The leader's basic assumptions concerning human behavior and human nature affect his actions, decisions, and other managerial practices.
10. Dissatisfaction among employees is often present, but difficult to isolate. The supervisor should seek to weaken dissatisfaction by keeping promises, being sincere and considerate, keeping employees informed, and so forth.
11. Constructive suggestions should be encouraged during the natural progress of the work.

E. Processes for Solving Problems
1. People find their daily tasks more meaningful and satisfying when they can improve them.
2. The causes of problems, or the key factors, are often hidden in the background. Ability to solve problems often involves the ability to isolate them from their backgrounds. There is some substance to the cliché that some persons "can't see the forest for the trees."
3. New procedures are often developed from old ones. Problems should be broken down into manageable parts. New ideas can be adapted from old one.
4. People think differently in problem-solving situations. Using a logical, patterned approach is often useful. One approach found to be useful includes these steps:
   a. Define the problem
   b. Establish objectives
   c. Get the facts
   d. Weigh and decide
   e. Take action
   f. Evaluate action

F. Training for Results
1. Participants respond best when they feel training is important to them.
2. The supervisor has responsibility for the training and development of those who report to him.
3. When training is delegated to others, great care must be exercised to insure the trainer has knowledge, aptitude, and interest for his work as a trainer.
4. Training (learning) of some type goes on continually. The most successful supervisor makes certain the learning contributes in a productive manner to operational goals.
5. New employees are particularly susceptible to training. Older employees facing new job situations require specific training, as well as having need for development and growth opportunities.
6. Training needs require continuous monitoring.
7. The training officer of an agency is a professional with a responsibility to assist supervisors in solving training problems.

8. Many of the self-development steps important to the supervisor's own growth are equally important to the development of peers and subordinates. Knowledge of these is important when the supervisor consults with others on development and growth opportunities.

G. Health, Safety, and Accident Prevention
1. Management-minded supervisors take appropriate measures to assist employees in maintaining health and in assuring safe practices in the work environment.
2. Effective safety training and practices help to avoid injury and accidents.
3. Safety should be a management goal. All infractions of safety which are observed should be corrected without exception.
4. Employees' safety attitude, training and instruction, provision of safe tools and equipment, supervision, and leadership are considered highly important factors which contribute to safety and which can be influenced directly by supervisors.
5. When accidents do occur, they should be investigated promptly for very important reasons, including the fact that information which is gained can be used to prevent accidents in the future.

H. Equal Employment Opportunity
1. The supervisor should endeavor to treat all employees fairly, without regard to religion, race, sex, or national origin.
2. Groups tend to reflect the attitude of the leader. Prejudice can be detected even in very subtle form. Supervisors must strive to create a feeling of mutual respect and confidence in every employee.
3. Complete utilization of all human resources is a national goal. Equitable consideration should be accorded women in the work force, minority-group members, the physically and mentally handicapped, and the older employee. The important question is: "Who can do the job?"
4. Training opportunities, recognition for performance, overtime assignments, promotional opportunities, and all other personnel actions are to be handled on an equitable basis.

I. Improving Communications
1. Communications is achieving understanding between the sender and the receiver of a message. It also means sharing information—the creation of understanding.
2. Communication is basic to all human activity. Words are means of conveying meanings; however, real meanings are in people.
3. There are very practical differences in the effectiveness of one-way, impersonal, and two-way communications. Words spoken face-to-face are better understood. Telephone conversations are effective, but lack the rapport of person-to-person exchanges. The whole person communicates.
4. Cooperation and communication in an organization go hand in hand. When there is a mutual respect between people, spelling out rules and procedures for communicating is unnecessary.
5. There are several barriers to effective communications. These include failure to listen with respect and understanding, lack of skill in feedback, and misinterpreting the meanings of words used by the speaker. It is also common

practice to listen to what we want to hear, and tune out things we do not want to hear.
6. Communication is management's chief problem. The supervisor should accept the challenge to communicate more effectively and to improve interagency and intra-agency communications.
7. The supervisor may often plan for and conduct meetings. The planning phase is critical and may determine the success or the failure of a meeting.
8. Speaking before groups usually requires extra effort. Stage fright may never disappear completely, but it can be controlled.

J. Self-Development
1. Every employee is responsible for his own self-development.
2. Toastmaster and toastmistress clubs offer opportunities to improve skills in oral communications.
3. Planning for one's own self-development is of vital importance. Supervisors know their own strengths and limitations better than anyone else.
4. Many opportunities are open to aid the supervisor in his developmental efforts, including job assignments; training opportunities, both governmental and non-governmental—to include universities and professional conferences and seminars.
5. Programmed instruction offers a means of studying at one's own rate.
6. Where difficulties may arise from a supervisor's being away from his work for training, he may participate in televised home study or correspondence courses to meet his self-development needs.

K. Teaching and Training
1. The Teaching Process
Teaching is encouraging and guiding the learning activities of students toward established goals. In most cases this process consists of five steps: preparation, presentation, summarization, evaluation, and application.

a. Preparation
Preparation is two-fold in nature; that of the supervisor and the employee. Preparation by the supervisor is absolutely essential to success. He must know what, when, where, how, and whom he will teach. Some of the factors that should be considered are:
1) The objectives
2) The materials needed
3) The methods to be used
4) Employee participation
5) Employee interest
6) Training aids
7) Evaluation
8) Summarization

Employee preparation consists in preparing the employee to receive the material. Probably the most important single factor in the preparation of the employee is arousing and maintaining his interest. He must know the objectives of the training, why he is there, how the material can be used, and its importance to him.

b. Presentation
   In presentation, have a carefully designed plan and follow it. The plan should be accurate and complete, yet flexible enough to meet situations as they arise. The method of presentation will be determined by the particular situation and objectives.

c. Summary
   A summary should be made at the end of every training unit and program. In addition, there may be internal summaries depending on the nature of the material being taught. The important thing is that the trainee must always be able to understand how each part of the new material relates to the whole.

d. Application
   The supervisor must arrange work so the employee will be given a chance to apply new knowledge or skills while the material is still clear in his mind and interest is high. The trainee does not really know whether he has learned the material until he has been given a chance to apply it. If the material is not applied, it loses most of its value.

e. Evaluation
   The purpose of all training is to promote learning. To determine whether the training has been a success or failure, the supervisor must evaluate this learning.
   In the broadest sense, evaluation includes all the devices, methods, skills, and techniques used by the supervisor to keep himself and the employees informed as to their progress toward the objectives they are pursuing. The extent to which the employee has mastered the knowledge, skills, and abilities, or changed his attitudes, as determined by the program objectives, is the extent to which instruction has succeeded or failed.
   Evaluation should not be confined to the end of the lesson, day, or program but should be used continuously. We shall note later the way this relates to the rest of the teaching process.

2. Teaching Methods
   A teaching method is a pattern of identifiable student and instructor activity used in presenting training material.
   All supervisors are faced with the problem of deciding which method should be used at a given time.

   a. Lecture
      The lecture is direct oral presentation of material by the supervisor. The present trend is to place less emphasis on the trainer's activity and more on that of the trainee.

   b. Discussion
      Teaching by discussion or conference involves using questions and other techniques to arouse interest and focus attention upon certain areas, and by doing so creating a learning situation. This can be one of the most

valuable methods because it gives the employees an opportunity to express their ideas and pool their knowledge.

    c. Demonstration
The demonstration is used to teach how something works or how to do something. It can be used to show a principle or what the results of a series of actions will be. A well-staged demonstration is particularly effective because it shows proper methods of performance in a realistic manner.

    d. Performance
Performance is one of the most fundamental of all learning techniques or teaching methods. The trainee may be able to tell how a specific operation should be performed but he cannot be sure he knows how to perform the operation until he has done so.
As with all methods, there are certain advantages and disadvantages to each method.

    e. Which Method to Use
Moreover, there are other methods and techniques of teaching. It is difficult to use any method without other methods entering into it. In any learning situation, a combination of methods is usually more effective than any one method alone.

Finally, evaluation must be integrated into the other aspects of the teaching-learning process.

It must be used in the motivation of the trainees; it must be used to assist in developing understanding during the training; and it must be related to employee application of the results of training.

This is distinctly the role of the supervisor.

HOUSING AND COMMUNITY DEVELOPMENT GLOSSARY

ACRONYMS AND ABBREVIATED REFERENCES

ACC	Annual contributions contract.
AHOP	Areawide housing opportunity plan.
AHS	Annual housing survey.
AML	Adjustable mortgage loan.
APA	Administrative Procedure Act (5 U.S.C. 551 et seq.)
ARM	Adjustable rate mortgage.
BMIR	Below-market interest rate.
Budget Act	Congressional Budget and Impoundment Control Act of 1974.
Budget Res.	Concurrent resolution on the budget.
CBO	Congressional Budget Office.
CD	Community development.
CDBG	Community development block grant.
CFR	Code of Federal Regulations.
CIAP	Comprehensive improvement assistance program.
Continuing Res	Joint resolution continuing appropriations for the next fiscal year.
CPI	Consumer Price Index.
DOE	Department of Energy.
EDA	Economic Development Administration.
EIS	Environmental impact statement.
ERTA	Economic Recovery Tax Act of 1981.
Fannie Mae	Federal National Mortgage Association.
FDIC	Federal Deposit Insurance Corporation.
FEMA	Federal Emergency Management Agency.
FFB	Federal Financing Bank.
FHA	Federal Housing Administration.
FHLBB	Federal Home Loan Bank Board.
FHLMC	Federal Home Loan Mortgage Corporation (Freddie Mac).
FmHA	Farmers Home Administration.
FMR	Fair market rent.
FNMA	Federal National Mortgage Association (Fannie Mae).
FR	Federal Register.
Freddie Mac	Federal Home Loan Mortgage Corporation.
FSLIC	Federal Savings and Loan Insurance Corporation.
GAO	Government Accounting Office.
Garn-St Germain	Garn-St Germain Depository Institutions Act of 1982.
GEM	Growing equity mortgage.
Ginnie Mae	Government National Mortgage Association.
GNMA	Government National Mortgage Association (Ginnie Mae).

GLOSSARY

GPM	Graduated payment mortgage.
Gramm-Latta	Omnibus Budget Reconciliation Act of 1981.
HAP	Housing assistance plan.
HFA	Housing finance agency.
HHS	Department of Health and Human Services.
HoDAG	Housing development grant.
HUD	Department of Housing and Urban Development.
HURRA	Housing and Urban-Rural Recovery Act of 1983.
IG	Inspector General.
IRS	Internal Revenue Service.
MBS	Mortgage-backed securities.
Mod Rehab	Moderate rehabilitation.
MPS	Minimum property standards.
MSA	Metropolitan statistical area.
NHP	National Housing Partnership.
NIBS	National Institute of Building Sciences.
NOFA	Notice of funding availability.
NSA	Neighborhood strategy area.
OBRA	Omnibus Budget Reconciliation Act of 1981.
OMB	Office of Management and Budget.
PAM	Pledged account mortgage.
PC	Participation certificate.
PFS	Performance funding system.
PHA	Public housing agency.
PLAM	Price-level adjusted mortgage.
PMI	Private mortgage insurance.
PUD	Planned unit development.
RAM	Reverse annuity mortgage.
RAP	Rental assistance payments.
REIT	Real estate investment trust.
RESPA	Real Estate Settlement Procedures Act of 1974.
SAM	Shared appreciation mortgage.
Solar Bank	Solar Energy and Energy Conservation Bank.
SRO	Single room occupancy housing.
Sub Rehab	Substantial rehabilitation.
TEFRA	Tax Equity and Fiscal Responsibility Act of 1982.
TMAP	Temporary mortgage assistance payments.
UDAG	Urban development action grant.
U.S.C	United States Code.
VA	Veterans' Administration.

ABBREVIATED STATUTORY CITATIONS

Sec. 5	United States Housing Act of 1937 (funding for public housing and section 8 housing).
Sec. 7(o)	Department of Housing and Urban Development Act (legislative review of HUD rules and regulations).

GLOSSARY

Sec. 8	United States Housing Act of 1937 (low-income rental housing assistance).
Sec. 9	United States Housing Act of 1937 (operating subsidies).
Sec. 14	United States Housing Act of 1937 (CLAP).
Sec. 17	United States Housing Act of 1937 (rental rehabilitation and development).
Sec. 101	Housing and Urban Development Act of 1965 (rent supplement).
Sec. 104	Housing and Community Development Act of 1974 (CDBG applications and review).
Sec. 105	Housing and Community Development Act of 1974 (CDBG eligible activities).
Sec. 106	Housing and Community Development Act of 1974 (CDBG allocation and distribution of funds).
Sec. 107	Housing and Community Development Act of 1974 (CD discretionary fund).
Sec. 108	Housing and Community Development Act of 1974 (CD loan guarantees).
Sec. 119	Housing and Community Development Act of 1974 (UDAG).
Sec. 201	Housing and Community Development Amendments of 1978 (troubled projects).
Sec. 202	Housing Act of 1959 (elderly and handicapped housing).
Sec. 203	Housing and Community Development Amendments of 1978 (management and preservation of HUD-owned projects). National Housing Act (single-family mortgage insurance).
Sec. 207	National Housing Act (multifamily mortgage insurance).
Sec. 213	Housing and Community Development Act of 1974 (allocation of funds for assisted housing). National Housing Act (cooperative housing mortgage insurance).
Sec. 221	National Housing Act (multifamily mortgage insurance).
Sec. 221(d)(3)	National Housing Act (BMIR rental housing mortgage insurance).
Sec. 231	National Housing Act (mortgage insurance for elderly and handicapped rental housing).
Sec. 235	National Housing Act (home mortgage interest reduction payments).
Sec. 236	National Housing Act (rental and cooperative housing interest reduction payments).
Sec. 302(b)(2)	Federal National Mortgage Association Charter Act (FNMA authority to deal in conventional mortgages).

GLOSSARY

Sec. 305(a)(2)	Federal Home Loan Mortgage Corporation Act (FHLMC authority to deal in conventional mortgages).
Sec. 312	Housing Act of 1964 (rehabilitation loans).
Sec. 502	Housing Act of 1949 (rural housing loans and loan guarantees).
Sec. 513	Housing Act of 1949 (rural housing authorization amounts).
Sec. 515	Housing Act of 1949 (elderly and handicapped rural housing).
Sec. 521	Housing Act of 1949 (rural housing loan interest credits and RAP).
Sec. 533	Housing Act of 1949 (housing preservation grants).
Title I	Housing and Community Development Act of 1974 (CDBG and UDAG). Housing Act of 1949 (urban renewal). National Housing Act (FHA property improvement loan insurance).
Title II	National Housing Act (FHA mortgage insurance).
Title V	Housing Act of 1949 (rural housing).

TERMS

Adjustable mortgage loan—See "adjustable rate mortgage".

Adjustable rate mortgage—A mortgage covering a loan the interest rate of which may vary periodically over the term of the loan, generally according to an established index. Also referred to as an adjustable mortgage loan.

Amortization—Gradual reduction of the principal of a loan, together with the payment of interest, according to a schedule of periodic payments so that the principal is fully paid by the end of the term of the loan.

Annual contributions contract—A contract under which HUD makes payments to a public housing agency equal to the amount of principal and interest owed by the PHA under obligations issued by it for the development, operation, or modernization of a public housing project.

Annual housing survey—An annual study by HUD and the Bureau of the Census regarding housing units, homeowners, and renters.

Appropriation—Constitutionally required legislation that grants Federal agencies the authority to make payments out of the Treasury for general or particular purposes. There are three general categories of appropriations legislation: general, supplemental, and continuing.

Areawide housing opportunity plan—A program to reduce the geographical concentration of lower income families by expanding housing opportunities throughout a wide area.

Assistance payments—Federal payments, made directly or through public housing agencies, to owners or prospective owners of rental housing to pay part of the rent of lower income tenants. See "interest-reduction payments".

Assumable mortgage—Mortgage in which the existing debt may be taken over by a third party without approval of the lender.

GLOSSARY

Authorization—Legislation granting authority for the congressional consideration of appropriations for general or particular purposes. Although unauthorized appropriations may be subject to points of order, they are legally valid if enacted.

Balloon mortgage—Mortgage under which the loan matures before the principal is fully repaid.

Below-market interest rate—HUD-insured mortgages financing homes for lower income families and displaced families bearing interest rates lower than the market rate, with the Federal Government bearing the cost of the difference in rates by purchase of the mortgages. See section 221(d)(3) of the National Housing Act.

Block grants—Grants by HUD on a noncategorical formula basis to assist community development and rehabilitation, including slum and blight elimination, conservation of housing, increased public services, improved use of land, and preservation of property. See title I of the Housing and Community Development Act of 1974.

Borrowing authority—Authority to incur indebtedness for which the Federal Government is liable, which authority is granted in advance of the provision of appropriations to repay such debts. Borrowing authority may take the form of authority to borrow from the Treasury or authority to borrow from the public by means of the sale of Federal agency obligations. Borrowing authority is not an appropriation since it provides a Federal agency only with the authority to incur a debt, and not the authority to make payments from the Treasury under the debt. Subsequent appropriations are required to liquidate the borrowing authority.

Budget authority—Legal authority to enter into obligations that will result in immediate or future outlays of Federal funds. Appropriations (unless liquidating borrowing authority or contract authority), contract authority, and borrowing authority are the three primary types of budget authority.

Coinsurance—HUD insurance of a mortgage, advance, or loan with the lender assuming a percentage of the loss on the insured obligation. See section 244 of the National Housing Act.

Commitment—An agreement to make or purchase a mortgage loan at a future date, or an agreement to insure a mortgage at a future date, if prescribed conditions are met by the mortgagee. Under HUD mortgage insurance, a traditional administration distinction exists between a special type of commitment known as a "conditional commitment" and other commitments known as "firm commitments". Under the former, a commitment is made to insure a mortgage (on a specific property for a definite loan amount) to be given by a future purchaser of the property involved if such a purchaser meets certain eligibility requirements. The term "standby commitment" is commonly used in the secondary market for residential mortgages to describe a commitment to purchase a mortgage loan or loans with specific terms, both parties understanding that the purchase is not likely to be completed unless particular circumstances make that advantageous to the seller of the mortgage. These commitments are typically used to enable the borrower to obtain construction financing at a lower cost on the assumption that permanent financing of the project will be available on more favorable terms than under the commitment when the project is completed and generating income.

Community development block grants—Block grants for community development made to States, urban counties, and metropolitan cities under section 106 of the Housing and Community Development Act of 1974.

GLOSSARY

Comprehensive improvement assistance—Assistance provided for the modernization of public housing projects under section 14 of the United States Housing Act of 1937.

Concurrent resolution on the budget—Concurrent resolution of the Congress establishing minimum revenues and maximum outlays for the congressional budget for the Federal Government.

Conditional commitment—See "commitment".

Condominiums—Multifamily housing projects with individual units owned by occupants, who also own an undivided interest in the common areas and facilities of the project.

Contract authority—Authority to enter into contracts obligating the Federal Government to make payments in the future, which authority is granted in advance of the provision of appropriations to make such payments. Contract authority is not an appropriation since it provides a Federal agency only with the authority to incur an obligation, and not the authority to make payments from the Treasury under the obligation. Subsequent appropriations are required to liquidate the contract authority.

Conventional mortgage—A mortgage covering a loan that is not insured by the HUD or guaranteed by the FmHA or VA.

Cooperatives—Multifamily housing projects owned by cooperative corporations with the stockholders of the corporations having the right to occupancy of the units.

Cost certification—A limitation, under HUD mortgage insurance for multifamily housing, on the amount of a mortgage eligible for insurance, which limitation is determined after completion of the project on the basis of the builder's certification as to the actual dollar amount of his costs for specific items of construction and prescribed related expenditures. Under this requirement, the insured mortgage is limited to a fixed percentage of that certified amount.

Deep subsidy program—Program of rental assistance payments under section 236(f)(2) of the National Housing Act.

Default—Failure to meet the terms of a mortgage or other loan agreement. Generally, a delinquency of more than 30 days under a mortgage is considered a default.

Delinquency—Failure to make any timely payment due under a mortgage or other loan agreement.

Direct endorsement—HUD program of delegated private mortgage processing of FHA loan applications under the single family mortgage insurance programs.

Discount point—An amount that may be payable to a lender by a borrower or seller in addition to principal and interest, equal to 1 percent of the principal amount of the loan.

Discretionary fund—Funds set aside for discretionary grants by HUD under section 107 of the Housing and Community Development Act of 1974.

Due-on-sale clause—A clause that may be included in a mortgage to authorize the mortgagee to require full repayment of the loan upon any transfer of the property.

Economic mix—Occupancy of rental housing by families of varying economic levels, including very low-income families, which is to be promoted by housing assistance payments. See section 8 of the United States Housing Act of 1937.

Elderly and handicapped housing—Generally refers to housing for elderly and handicapped persons developed by nonprofit sponsors with assistance provided by HUD under section 202 of the Housing Act of 1959.

GLOSSARY

Entitlement community—An urban county or metropolitan city eligible to receive a community development block grant directly from HUD.

Environmental impact statements—Statements required to be made under section 102(2)(C) of the National Environmental Policy Act of 1969 by Federal agencies in their recommendations or reports on proposals for legislation and other major Federal actions significantly affecting the quality of the human environment, as to the environmental impact of the proposed action; any adverse environmental effects that cannot be avoided should the proposal be implemented; relationship between local short-term use of man's environment and the maintenance and enhancement of long-term productivity; and any irreversible or irretrievable commitments of resources that would be involved in the proposed action should it be implemented. Applicants for block grants can assume responsibility for this statement under the community development program. See section 104(f) of the Housing and Community Development Act of 1974.

Estimated value—The basis of one of the limits on the amount of a mortgage that can be insured by HUD. For example, under certain programs the mortgage may not exceed 90 percent of the estimated value of the property when completed.

Fair market rent—An amount determined by HUD to be the cost of modest rental units in a particular market area.

Federal Home Loan Mortgage Corporation—A federally established and sponsored corporation, under the supervision of the Federal Home Loan Bank Board, that provides a secondary market primarily for conventional mortgages.

Federal Housing Administration—Part of HUD that has responsibility for carrying out the mortgage insurance programs of the National Housing Act.

Federal National Mortgage Association—A federally established and sponsored private corporation, under the general supervision of HUD, that provides a secondary market for mortgages.

Firm commitment—See "commitment".

Fiscal year—Annual accounting period of the Federal Government, beginning October 1 and ending September 30 of the subsequent calendar year. The fiscal year is designated by the calendar year in which it ends, so that fiscal year 2005 refers to the fiscal year beginning October 1, 2004 and ending September 30, 2005.

Flood insurance program—Program under which FEMA makes flood insurance available to participating communities under the National Flood Insurance Act of 1968.

Forebearance—The act of postponing or refraining from taking legal action against a mortgagor even though mortgage payments are in arrears.

Foreclosure—Legal procedure under which the property securing a loan is sold to pay the debt owed by a borrower who has defaulted.

Government National Mortgage Association—Federal corporation, and part of HUD, that provides a secondary market for federally guaranteed mortgages.

Graduated payment mortgage—A mortgage under which payments are comparatively low initially and then increase over a specified period before reaching a constant level.

Ground lease—Lease of land without improvements.

Growing equity mortgage—Mortgage under which payments increase over a specified period in order to accelerate the repayment of principal and thereby shorten the term of the loan.

Guaranteed loan—Loan in which a private lender is assured repayment by the Federal Government of part or all of the principal or interest, or both, in the event of a

GLOSSARY

default by the borrower. Unlike an insured loan, no insurance fund exists and no insurance premiums are paid.

Hold-harmless provision—Statutory provision ensuring the continued eligibility of a specified class for certain assistance for a limited period of time. The most commonly cited examples are contained in paragraphs (4) and (6) of section 102(a) of the Housing and Community Development Act of 1974.

Home equity conversion mortgage—A form of mortgage in which the lender makes periodic payments to the borrower using the borrower's equity in the home as security.

Housing allowance payments—Payments made by HUD under section 504 of the Housing Act of 1970 to assist families in meeting rental or homeownership expenses.

Housing assistance planA part of the CDBG application describing local housing conditions and sets quantitative goals for providing housing to low- and moderate-income residents.

Housing development grant—Grant made by HUD under section 17(d) of the United States Housing Act of 1937 for the new construction or substantial rehabilitation of rental housing.

Housing finance agency—State agency responsible for financing housing and administering assisted housing programs.

Housing preservation grant—Grant made by FmHA under section 533 of the Housing Act of 1949 for the rehabilitation of single-family housing, rental housing, or cooperatives for low- and very low-income families and persons.

Industrial revenue bond—A debt instrument issued by a municipality or development corporation to finance the development of revenue-producing projects. Project revenues are then used to pay the debt service on the bonds. Section 103(b) of the Internal Revenue Code of 1954 establishes certain limitations.

Installment land contract—See "land contract".

Insured loan—Loan in which a private lender is assured repayment by the Federal Government of part or all of the principal or interest, or both, and for which the borrower pays insurance premiums.

Interest rate credits—Generally refers to the FmHA program of subsidized interest rate loans for single-family and multifamily housing for low or moderate income families under section 521(a)(1)(B) of the Housing Act of 1949. The subsidy may reduce the interest rate to as low as 1 percent.

Interest reduction payments—Periodic assistance payments by HUD to mortgagees to permit lower interest rate payments by lower income families (varying with fluctuations in incomes) on HUD insured mortgages financing homes, rental housing, or cooperative housing. See sections 235 and 236 of the National Housing Act.

Land contract—An agreement to transfer title to a property upon fulfillment of the contract conditions. Under an "installment land contract", the purchaser assumes possession immediately and makes periodic payments to the vendor (the owner of the property); title is transferred only when all payments have been made.

Leased housing—Low-rent housing provided by public housing agencies in housing leased from private owners.

Leveraging—The maximization of the effect of Federal assistance for a project by obtaining additional project funding from non-Federal sources. See section 119 of the Housing and Community Development Act of 1974.

Lien—Any legal claim on a property for payment of a debt. A mortgage is one example.

GLOSSARY

Loan-to-value ratio—The relationship between the amount of the mortgage loan and the appraised value of the property involved, expressed as a percentage of the appraised value. It is one of the traditional limitations on a mortgage eligible for mortgage insurance.

Lower income family—Generally, a family whose income does not exceed 80 percent of the median family income of the area involved.

Manufactured home—Housing, including a mobile home, that is factory-built or prefabricated.

Market rent—Rental that would be charged by the owner of a HUD-insured multifamily dwelling unit if the owner were paying interest on the loan at the HUD-approved market interest rate.

Metropolitan city—For purposes of the CDBG program, a city that is the central city of a metropolitan area or that has a population of not less than 50,000.

Metropolitan statistical area—Metropolitan area defined by the Office of Management and Budget. Previously referred to as standard metropolitan statistical area.

Minimum property standards—HUD regulations establishing minimum acceptable standards for properties to be purchased with HUD-insured mortgage loans.

Moderate income family—For purposes of the CDBG program, a family whose income exceeds 50 percent of the median family income of the area involved, but does not exceed 80 percent of the median family income of the area.

Moderate rehabilitation—Rehabilitation that is less comprehensive than substantial rehabilitation, such as repair or replacement of the heating or electrical system of a project.

Modernization—See "comprehensive improvement assistance".

Mortgage—Conveyance of an interest in real property as security for repayment of a loan, including a loan made for the purchase or improvement of the real property.

Mortgage-backed securities—Obligations issued by an organization that has held and set aside mortgages as security for payment of the obligations. FNMA, GNMA, and FHLMC, as well as private organizations, issue such obligations.

Mortgage insurance programs—Generally refers to the insured loan programs carried out by HUD, through the FHA, under the National Housing Act.

Mortgage revenue bonds—Tax-exempt bonds issued by State and local governments and agencies to finance the sale or repair of single-family housing. The bonds are payable from revenues derived from repayments of interest on the mortgage loans financed from the proceeds of the bonds. Section 103A of the Internal Revenue Code of 1954 establishes certain limitations. Referred to as mortgage subsidy bonds in the Internal Revenue Code of 1954.

Mortgagee—A lender who is conveyed an interest in real property under a mortgage.

Mortgagor—A borrower who conveys an interest in real property under a mortgage.

Multifamily housingGenerally a project containing dwelling units for more than 4 families.

National Housing Partnership—A private limited partnership established under title IX of the Housing and Urban Development Act of 1969 for the purpose of carrying out the building, maintenance, or rehabilitation of housing and related facilities for lower or moderate income families. It can enter into partnerships or joint ventures, conduct research, provide technical assistance, and make loans or grants to accomplish its purpose.

GLOSSARY

National Institute of Building Sciences—A nonprofit nongovernmental organization established under section 809 of the Housing and Community Development Act of 1974 to make findings and to advise public and private sectors of the economy with respect to the use of building science and technology in achieving nationally acceptable standards for use in housing and building regulations.

Negative amortization—A loan prepayment schedule under which payments do not cover the full amount of interest due. The unpaid interest is added to the principal and, as a result, the outstanding principal balance increases rather than decreases.

Neighborhood development grant—A grant made by HUD to an eligible neighborhood nonprofit organization under section 123 of the Housing and Urban-Rural Recovery Act of 1983 to assist the organization in carrying out certain neighborhood development activities.

Neighborhood strategy area—Area in which concentrated housing rehabilitation and community development block grant activities are being undertaken.

Nonentitlement area—For purposes of the CDBG program, an area that is neither a metropolitan city nor urban county, and is therefore generally ineligible for direct grants from HUD.

Nonprofit sponsor—A group organized to undertake a housing project for reasons other than making a profit.

Notice of funding availability—A notice by HUD to inform potential project sponsors that contract authority is available.

Off-budget program—Federal program the transactions of which are not included in the Budget of the United States Government as a result of statutory requirement.

Operating subsidies—HUD payments to public housing agencies to assist the payment of operating expenses of public housing, or to the owners of certain multifamily projects for low income families. See section 9 of the United States Housing Act of 1937.

Participation loan—Loans made by the FmHA or others when another lender makes part of the loan.

Pass through—Principal and interest receipts on housing mortgages are "passed through" by GNMA, FNMA, FHLMC, or other organizations to the purchasers of their securities or obligations that have been sold and secured by the mortgages set aside as security for the obligations.

Planned unit development—Development and construction of a residential community as a unit in accordance with a plan for the entire development.

Pledged account mortgage—A graduated payment mortgage in which part of the buyer's down payment is deposited in a savings account. Funds are drawn from the account to supplement the buyer's monthly payments during the early years of the loan.

Pocket of poverty—For purposes of the UDAG program, a contiguous area of particularly severe poverty in a city or urban county. A city or urban county that fails to meet the general eligibility standards for UDAG assistance may be eligible if it contains such an area.

Prepayment penalty—A penalty that may be levied for repayment of a loan before it falls due.

Price-level adjusted mortgage—Mortgage under which the outstanding balance is adjusted according to an established price index, while the interest rate remains fixed.

Principal—The amount of debt, exclusive of accrued interest, remaining on a loan. Before any principal has been repaid, the total loaned amount is the principal.

GLOSSARY

Private mortgage insurance—Insurance by private companies of lenders against losses on mortgage loans.

Program reservation—HUD action reserving funds for a specific approved public housing project. This reservation is subject to PHA fulfillment of all HUD requirements.

Public housing—Lower income housing owned and operated by a public housing agency and assisted under the United States Housing Act of 1937 (other than under section 8 or 17).

Public housing agency—Public agency established by a State or local government to finance or operate low-income housing assisted under the United States Housing Act of 1937.

Real estate investment trust—A trust established by real estate investors primarily for the management and control of investments in mortgages and to sell obligations secured by mortgages and property held by the trust.

Recapture—Requiring repayment of assistance provided, either because the assistance has not been used within a certain period of time or a specified event (such as the sale of assisted property) occurs that permits repayment of all or a part of the assistance. See section 235(c)(2) of the National Housing Act.

Refinancing—Payment of a loan with amounts borrowed under a new loan.

Rehabilitation—The improvement or repair of property. Such term includes substantial and moderate rehabilitation, but excludes new construction.

Rehabilitation loans—Loans made by HUD under section 312 of the Housing Act of 1964 for the rehabilitation of property.

Reinsurance—Program under section 249 of the National Housing Act to demonstrate possible advantages of having private mortgage insurance companies enter into reinsurance contracts with HUD, under which such private insurers would assume a percentage of the risk on certain single-family mortgages insured by HUD.

Rent control—Limitation of annual rent increases by municipal ordinance, State, or Federal law.

Rent supplements—Annual Federal payments to owners of housing built with certain HUD mortgage insurance on behalf of prescribed types of lower income families.

Rental assistance payments—Generally refers to the FmHA program of rental assistance for low income families in rural areas under section 521(a)(2)(A) of the Housing Act of 1949.

Replacement cost—The basis of one of the limits placed on the amount of a mortgage that can be insured by HUD under certain programs, such as the mortgage may not exceed 90 percent of replacement cost of the housing when completed.

Reverse annuity mortgage—See "home equity conversion mortgage".

Rural area—A non-urban area meeting the requirements of section 520 of the Housing Act of 1949 and eligible assistance under the FmHA housing programs.

Second mortgage—A mortgage that grants rights subordinate to the rights granted by the initial mortgage. A second mortgage generally bears a higher rate of interest than the initial mortgage to reflect the greater risk of the lender.

Secondary mortgage market—Nationwide market for the purchase and sale of mortgages. FHLMC, FNMA, and GNMA are the 3 federally established entities that purchase mortgages in the secondary mortgage market, thereby increasing the availabilty of funds to financial institutions for additional residential loans.

Seed money—Advances, loans, or grants to cover preliminary expenses of constructing housing projects, such as the cost of planning and obtaining financing.

GLOSSARY

Shared appreciation mortgage—Mortgage under which the borrower receives financial assistance in purchasing a property and agrees in return to give the lender a portion of the future increase in the value of the property.

Shared housing—Generally refers to arrangements under which elderly and handicapped persons share the facilities of a dwelling with others in order to meet their housing needs and reduce the costs of housing. See section 8(p) of the United States Housing Act of 1937.

Single-family housing—Generally a structure containing dwelling units for 1 to 4 families.

Single room occupancy housing—Residential properties in which some or all dwelling units do not contain bathroom or kitchen facilities. See section 8(n) of the United States Housing Act of 1937.

Small city—A city that does not qualify as a metropolitan city for purposes of receiving a community development block grant under section 106 of the Housing and Community Development Act of 1974.

Standby commitment—See "commitment".

Substantial rehabilitationImprovements of a property from substandard to safe and sanitary conditions. It can vary from gutting and reconstruction to accumulated deferred maintenance. It may also involve conversion of nonresidential property to residential use.

Supplemental loans—HUD-insured loans under section 241 of the National Housing Act for improvements or additions to multifam-ily housing, nursing homes, group practice facilities, or hospitals.

Tandem plan purchases—The purchase by GNMA of certain housing mortgages at higher prices than would be paid by FNMA, FHLMC or other mortgage purchasers, with subsequent resale by GNMA at the best price obtainable, or as back-up of GNMA's mortgage-backed securities. The term derives from the original practice of FNMA purchasing from GNMA "in tandem" with the GNMA purchase.

Temporary mortgage assistance payments—Mortgage assistance payments authorized to be made under section 230(a) of the National Housing Act to a mortgagor of a single-family residence who defaults on the mortgage due to circumstances beyond the mortgagor's control. Constitutes an alternative to acquisition of the mortgage by HUD under section 230(b) of the National Housing Act.

Tenant contribution—The monthly amount of rent required to be paid by a tenant receiving rental assistance under a Federal housing program. Currently is 30 percent of monthly adjusted family income. See section 3(a) of the United States Housing Act of 1937.

Total development costs—The sum of all HUD-approved costs for planning, administration, site acquisition, relocation, demolition, construction and equipment, interest and carrying charges, on-site streets and utilities, nondwelling facilities, a contingency allowance, insurance premiums, off-site facilities, any initial operating deficit, and all other costs necessary to develop the project.

Troubled housing—Rental or cooperative housing project receiving assistance from HUD under section 201 of the Housing and Community Development Amendments of 1978 to restore financial soundness, improve management, and maintain the low and moderate income character of the project.

GLOSSARY

Turnkey housing—Housing initially financed and built by private sponsors and purchased upon completion by public housing agencies for use by lower income families under the public housing program.

Unit of general local government—A general purpose political subdivision of a State, such as a county, city, township, town, or village.

Urban county—For purposes of the CDBG and UDAG programs, generally refers to a county in a metropolitan area that has a combined population of not less than 200,000.

Urban development action grant—A grant made to an urban county, city, or unincorporated portion of an urban county under section 119 of the Housing and Community Development Act of 1974.

Urban homesteading—Program of HUD transfers of unoccupied residences under section 810 of the Housing and Community Development Act of 1974 to individuals or families without any substantial consideration where the individuals or families agree to occupy the residences not less than 5 years and to make repairs and improvements required to meet health and safety standards within certain time limits. Under a demonstration multifamily homestead-ing program, HUD transfers properties to local governments for conversion or rehabilitation to use primarily as housing for lower income families.

Urban renewal—Elimination and prevention of the development or spread of slums and blight, including slum clearance and redevelopment, or rehabilitation and conservation, assisted by HUD advances, loans, and grants under title I of the Housing Act of 1949. Program is being terminated under the provisions of title I of the Housing and Community Development Act of 1974.

Usury laws—Laws limiting the maximum rate of interest that may be charged on a loan.

Vacancy rate—In reference to dwelling units, the percentage of the total dwelling units in an area that are vacant and available for residence.

Variable interest rate—A means by which a lender is permitted to adjust the interest rate on a loan to reflect changes in the prime rateusually within a prescribed range and with advanced notice.

Very low-income family—Generally, a family whose income does not exceed 50 percent of the median family income of the area involved.

Voucher demonstration—Demonstration program of rental assistance under section 8(o) of the United States Housing Act of 1937. Assistance payments are provided for an eligible family based on the difference between the payment standard established by the Secretary for the area involved and 30 percent of the family's monthly adjusted income. The tenant contribution is the difference between the rent negotiated by the family and the amount of the monthly assistance payment.

www.ingramcontent.com/pod-product-compliance
Lightning Source LLC
Chambersburg PA
CBHW081828300426
44116CB00014B/2508